true green kids

Photo: Corbis Australia

true green kids

100 things you can do to save the planet

Kim McKay and Jenny Bonnin

WASHINGTON, D.C.

First U.S. Edition published by National Geographic Society
First Australian edition published in April 2008 by ABC Books for the
AUSTRALIAN BROADCASTING CORPORATION
GPO Box 9994 Sydney NSW 2001

For more information, please call 1-800-NGS LINE (647-5463) or write to the following address: National Geographic Society/ 1145 17th Street N.W., Washington, D.C. 20036-4688 U.S.A.

Printed in U.S.A.

Trade paperback ISBN 978-1-4263-0442-2
Reinforced library edition ISBN 978-1-4263-0443-9

Design, illustrations and image selection by Marian Kyte
Research and editing by Russell Thomson
U.S. adaptation by Kathy Stark
Color reproduction by Graphic Print Group, Adelaide

A percentage of proceeds from the sale of *True Green Kids* benefits Clean Up the World.

National Geographic has purchased carbon credits to neutralize emissions produced by the printing of this book.

Cover photo: Chris Bennett.

Image graphics: Marian Kyte.

Library of Congress Cataloging-in-Publication data available from the publisher upon request.

Visit us online at www.nationalgeographic.com/books
For librarians and teachers: www.ngchildrensbooks.com
More for kids from National Geographic:
kids.nationalgeographic.com

For information about special discounts for bulk purchases, please contact National Geographic Books Special Sales: ngspecsales@ngs.org

For rights or permissions inquiries, please contact National Geographic Books Subsidiary Rights: ngbookrights@ngs.org

Founded in 1888, the National Geographic Society is one of the largest nonprofit scientific and educational organizations in the world. It reaches more than 285 million people worldwide each month through its official journal, NATIONAL GEOGRAPHIC, and its four other magazines; the National Geographic Channel; television documentaries; radio programs; films; books; videos and DVDs; maps; and interactive media. National Geographic has funded more than 8,000 scientific research projects and supports an education program combating geographic illiteracy.

This book is printed on recycled paper and its production has been carbon offset by CO_2 Australia. For more National Geographic "green" books and initiatives, visit: www.preserveourplanet.com.

contents

foreword 7

introduction 8

in your room 10

at home 22

outdoors 34

with friends 46

buying stuff 58

at school 70

teamwork 82

on vacation 94

fun things to make 106

true green facts 118

acknowledgments 143

cool resources

132 eco quiz

134 websites

138 glossary

141 clean up the world

141 adventure ecology

Photo: Tourism Tasmania and Anthony Palmer

Photo: Adam Broomberg and Oliver Chanarin

foreword

David de Rothschild
Founder, Adventure Ecology;
National Geographic Fellow; and
Clean Up the World Ambassador
www.adventureecology.com

My adventures in some of the planet's most spectacular, exciting, and environmentally important locations—from the lush wildness of the Amazon to the cloud-hidden summits of the Himalayas, from the deep, cool, dark blue waters of our Pacific to the breathtaking endless horizons of our polar regions—have inspired me to do my part for the health of our planet. I'm so passionate about it that sometimes I think I might just pop. Rather than let all that excitement disappear, I decided to share my stories and create Adventure Ecology, a web-based network that works alongside another group of people who not only represent the future leaders and visionaries of our planet, but who also have more passion, energy, and motivation than anyone else ... yup you guessed it, I am talking about YOU!

Now you've probably read the headlines and seen the TV reports. It seems we haven't been the best house guests, and as a result Planet Earth has caught a fever. Or as your friendly scientist may put it, the climate's changing. Our climate records now show that the six warmest years in the past 150 have all occurred since 1998. This evidence, and an understanding that we have been driving this changing climate, also tells us this is a problem that's clearly within our power to address. So rather than take the easy option and bury our heads in the sand, the time has come for all of us to tackle this environmental health crisis head-on and start doing our bit for the planet.

You might be thinking, "I can't even clean up my room, so how do you expect me to clean up the planet?" Well, with a bit of passion, imagination, and the right preparation, adventures can begin in unexpected places.

Being true green doesn't mean wearing funny-colored clothes that make you itch, or having to chain yourself, your friends, and the family pet to a tree (although that can be fun). Thanks to the great work of authors Kim and Jenny and the team at Clean Up the World, it now actually means the complete opposite. *True Green Kids* is so crammed full of fun, easy, and, more importantly, cool ways you can become an agent of change that rising to the challenge of protecting Planet Earth has become an exciting adventure rather than a chore. Once you start exploring and acting on the simple and practical actions presented throughout the book, you just won't look back.

So what's your adventure for our planet? Remember, the actions you take—alongside millions of others worldwide—WILL make a very big difference toward the future health of our home, Planet Earth. So let's get started!

introduction

Kim McKay and Jenny Bonnin

it's awesome!

When you look at the sky, do you ever wonder what is out there beyond the stars? The entire universe is so vast, so complex, and so amazing, it's easy to be overwhelmed by it all.

Sometimes it can make us ask questions about how we live our lives on this unique blue planet. Where do we fit in this picture?

We know that we can't live on any other planet yet—at least not the ones that are closest to us. Astronauts have been to the moon, and NASA's probes have checked out Mars and the moons of Saturn and Jupiter. There doesn't seem to be any water or atmosphere that would enable us to survive in these places, even if we could get there.

Would you believe us if we told you that we are using so many of Earth's resources to provide all the things we think we need that if we're not careful, one planet won't be enough for us?

Right now scientists all over the world are realizing the same thing. Something we hadn't been expecting to happen is underway. The way we live is affecting the delicate balance of the Earth's atmosphere.

The number of people on the planet has been growing steadily for thousands of years. But the number of people living today has created such pressure on the land, sea, and atmosphere that we have arrived at a tipping point. We use too much energy. We use too many resources. Our agriculture, industry, and vehicles pollute our skies—although on a bright sunny day you may still find that hard to believe. Climate has always been changeable, but now it is changing too fast, and we, the people of Planet Earth, seem to be the cause. We need to help slow down that change and start to repair the damage done.

In this book we will show you wonderful places that we all need to take care of, such as the Grand Canyon, the Everglades, our barrier islands, and our national parks. Most of these magnificent natural areas are now protected under conservation laws because they are unique to our country and deeply significant to Native Americans who have cared for this country for thousands of years. Amazing

This book is for you. The world is in your hands now. You are the next caretakers of the planet. Despite the damage that has been done to the Earth, it is not too late to fix it. That's why we're involved with Clean Up the World. We believe each of us can make a difference.

Tread lightly on the Earth. Remember we don't own the land, we belong to it.

It's up to us. It's up to you.

plants and animals live in these areas, but many are now endangered; some even face extinction as a result of climate change.

It's up to us to make sure that not only all those amazing sites but also a sustainable world is preserved for all of us. One day you will want to travel and see these wonders for yourself—the polar regions with their great whales and bears, or the wild plains of Africa with their elephants and wildebeest, or the Amazon, the most important rain forest in the world with so many different plants and animals we still don't really know all that's there.

In this book we've come up with lots of ideas on how you can help save the planet. Drive your parents crazy by reminding them to turn off the TV for a change! Swap clothes with friends. Grow food instead of buying it, and have many hours of fun exploring true green websites and trying out our eco-activities. There are also great ideas for things to make and do at school. And we would love to hear about what you are doing to make the world true green so we can put it on our website: www.betruegreen.com. Email us at getstarted@betruegreen.com.

Photos: far left, Chris Bennett: top, Kate Whitney Lucey

believe it or not...

The United States has the highest rate of carbon emissions in the world, with close to 6 billion tons of carbon dioxide (CO_2) gas released every year, more than 80 tons per household. To help you understand how much gas that is, one pound of CO_2 fills a balloon about two-and-one-half-feet wide, so in one year an American family of four would fill 160,000 balloons—enough to fill a building 27 stories tall and 100 feet square!

The challenge for all of us is to change the way we live. To start, we need to rely less on coal-fired power for our energy. Beyond that, we need to use less stuff, use things up, and wear them out before throwing them away. And we need to recycle as much as possible of whatever we do throw away. That way we will not only reduce the amount of energy needed to produce all that stuff, we will also reduce the amount of trash that ends up in landfills.

Your room is your very own world—it's a microcosm of the Earth. If you threw trash on the floor and never cleaned it up, your room would soon become a messy, unhealthy place to be. Take care of your environment, and it will take care of you by keeping you happy and healthy. Same goes for the planet.

in your room

1

be true green

You might think that there's not much you can do about big issues like global warming and climate change. But even small changes matter. One person can make a difference. If you and your family can make your lifestyle more sustainable, that's a start. If you can spread the true green message to your friends and their families and get your school and local community involved, then that's real progress. Just as every drop of water is precious and important, so are you. Be aware of the water and energy you use every day, eat fresh food, be healthy, be you, be true green!

Read this book, then make a list of the things—even little, everyday things—you can do that will help improve our environment and make our planet a healthier one.

Photo: Corbis Australia

your room

2

You can make your room a happier and healthier place just by adding some plants. They are nature's great air purifiers—removing carbon dioxide and harmful chemicals from the air, as well as adding oxygen. The air we breathe today was first produced 2.5 billion years ago when primitive plants started producing oxygen by photosynthesis. Plants take energy from the sun, carbon dioxide from the air, and water and minerals from the soil. They breathe out oxygen and water vapor. You'd need hundreds of plants in your room to provide all your oxygen, but just a couple will help keep the air clean.

Ask your grown-ups if there is a plant in your house that you can keep in your room, and decorate the pot.

Photo: Corbis Australia. Inset: Marian Kyte

3

let the sunshine in

The sun is the greatest source of energy we know. There are many ways to make the best use of natural light in your room. During the day, open the curtains to let as much light in as possible, and switch off the electric light. Move your desk closer to a window if possible. You can also make use of the sun's energy with a solar-powered battery charger, which captures the sunlight and converts it into energy that will power many kinds of batteries, including those used for iPods, laptop computers, and flashlights.

Fact: Enough sunlight falls on the Earth's surface every hour to meet the world's energy demands for an entire year.

Ask for a solar charger as a present. Use it to power your battery-charged toys and devices.

Photo: Corbis Australia. Illustration: Lachlan Chang

winter warmth 4

Do you like to snuggle up in bed with your favorite book on a cold winter's night? Rather than turning the heat up, why not add an extra blanket? If you live in a really cold area, use an electric blanket instead of a room heater; it will use less energy. Don't forget to close the curtains at night to keep the warmth in. On sunny days, open your curtains to let the sun warm your room. Sealing the gaps around your windows (and your door if it's cold in the hall) not only keeps you warmer in winter, but keeps the heat out in summer as well.

Make a fun draft stopper to keep those sneaky drafts out of your room. Visit http://www.craftbits.com/viewProject.do?projectID=516.

Photo: Chris Bennett

5 go surfing

discover

games

You only have to type "environment" into a search engine, and more than 400 million links pop up! So how do you choose which sites to investigate? There are lots of links in our special website section on pages 134–137, but to get the big picture, go to www.earth.google.com and see what you can find out just by looking at our wonderful planet.

Go green surfing, and make a list of all the websites there are, just for kids, that give you ideas about how to be eco-friendly. Share the list with your friends so that they can do their part, too. And don't forget to look for green games. There are a lot out there!

6

When you are not using your computer but don't want to switch it off, put it into "sleep" mode, and it will use less than 5 percent of its full power. If you have a phone charger, radio, DVD player, iPod, or MP3 player, unplug them at the outlet. An average American family can save around $100 a year simply by unplugging appliances and chargers when they're not being used.

Find out how to put your computer to sleep, and download the Earth Hour screensaver at http://usefulscreensaver.com.au. Learn more about Earth Hour by visiting www.earthhourus.org.

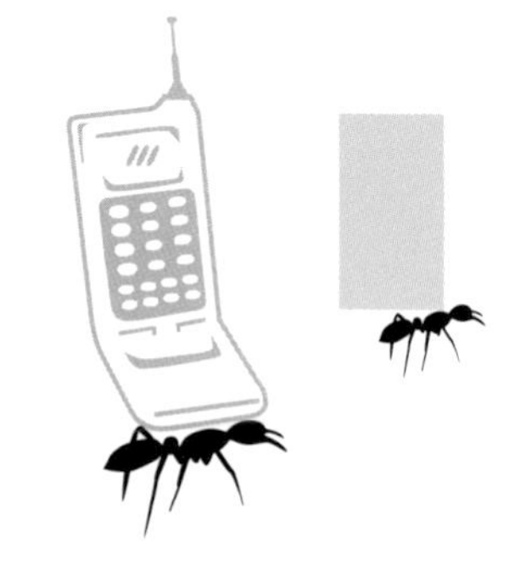

7

the recycling bug

If you reduce the amount of paper you use, you can cut down on waste, save the forests, and save money. Don't just throw paper away: reuse it and recycle it. Create a funky paper tray to sit on your desk so you can use both sides of every sheet—use the back for jotting down notes and making lists. Make a paper recycling container out of an old carton, and when it's full, empty it into the household recycling bin. Show your family how to re-use their paper by using both sides of every sheet, and how to properly recycle their waste paper and other items.

Find out how to recycle e-waste in your neighborhood by checking out your town's or city's website.

Illustration: Marian Kyte

8

get recharged

How many batteries do you use in your toys, MP3 player, watch, and cell phone in a year? Multiply that by the number of people who use batteries and you can see why an awful lot of batteries go into the trash. In fact, more than 621 tons of household batteries are thrown away in the United States every year! Batteries contain heavy metals that can soak into the ground and pollute water supplies. Rechargeable batteries may cost more, but they can be recharged and reused thousands of times, too. When possible, buy hand-operated items—such as wind-up radios—that function without batteries.

Make a list of everything you have that uses batteries to show how many batteries you are using. How can you decrease that number? What items can you do without?

Illustration: Marian Kyte

9

turn that music up!

Many rock groups and musicians are involved in spreading the word about the environment. Willie Nelson, Dave Matthews Band, and Bonnie Raitt are some of the best known. Live Earth concerts were held all around the world in 2007 to make people focus on the future of the planet and be aware of the problems that have to be solved. Many classical composers—including Beethoven and Vivialdi—wrote their greatest works in response to nature and the world around them. So listen to music that reminds you what a fascinating world we live in—and be inspired to make a difference!

Be "in tune" with the bands that help communicate a green message. Do you know if your favorite singers and bands are taking steps to help the environment? Write them a letter and ask them!

Photo: Corbis Australia

10

be a quick-change artist

What do you do when you've grown too big for your clothes, or you're tired of them? Do you pass them on to a younger brother or sister or take them to your local consignment shop? Here's another idea. Why not get together with a group of friends and organize a clothes-swapping party? Everyone brings some good-quality clothes they want to trade. It's also fun to be creative with your old clothes by adding some fabric paint or embroidery to them. There are lots of ways to customize them and give them new life.

Reuse and recycle your clothes—organize a clothes-swapping party!

Illustration: Marian Kyte

You can make your home true green. Think about your actions and how they impact the environment. Saving energy can help save *your* planet, so cut your electricity use, care for plants and pets, don't waste water, and recycle everything you can. And get your family on board so everyone can work together.

at home

11

save water

Because of changes to our atmosphere, our climate is changing. You've probably seen stories in the news about crazy storms or unusual weather patterns—well, one of those is drought, which is occurring in many areas of the country. It is up to all of us to find ways to save water. The average U.S. household uses 127,400 gallons of water a year—enough for 5 families to drain an Olympic-size swimming pool every year! Almost 60 percent is used in the bathroom, 20 percent for washing our clothes, and about 10 percent in the kitchen. Then there's watering the yard, washing the car—even filling swimming pools. Where better to start saving water than at home?

Use a bucket to make your own rainwater tank. Collect water when it rains and then use it on your yard and houseplants.

Photo: Chris Bennett. Graphics: Marian Kyte

12 smile!

Dentists recommend brushing your teeth for three to four minutes after every meal. Some people like to leave the faucet running while they clean their teeth, but doing that uses about 3 gallons of water per minute. So if you brush three times a day, you could use 50 gallons of water—that's more than 20 buckets a day! The water going down the sink does nothing to make your teeth cleaner—so just wet your brush, fill a glass for rinsing, and turn off the tap.

Remember: Turn off the faucet when you brush your teeth!

Photo: Marian Kyte

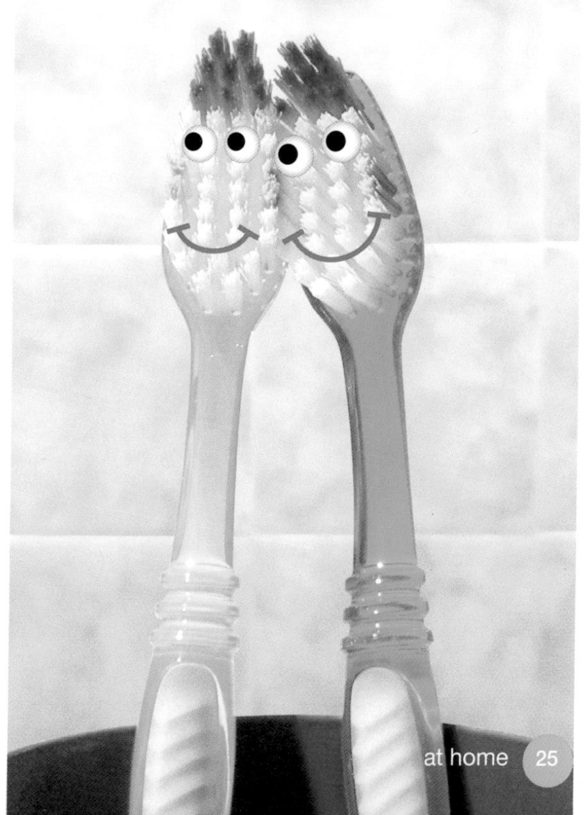

13

four-minute showers

If you cut your shower time from 7 minutes, which is the average, to 4, you could save more than 6,600 gallons of water a year! Buy a simple timer to stick on the bathroom wall to let you know when 4 minutes is up. Maybe you could reduce your shower time by a minute per week for a month and run a fun competition among your family to see who can have the shortest shower (and still be clean, of course!). You'll also save a lot of energy (and time and money) by using less hot water.

Keep a bucket in the bathroom to collect water while you are waiting for the shower to get hot, and use the water on the garden or yard.

Illustration: Marian Kyte

14

squeaky clean

We all use soap and other products to keep ourselves clean and beautiful. Many toiletries and cosmetics contain chemicals that can cause health problems, not only for people but for the Earth as well. Even if they don't bother you, their effect on the environment can be harmful, so use natural products whenever you can.

Look at the labels on some of the bottles in your bathroom and see for yourself just what's in them. Download your own "Dirty Dozen" card of ingredients to avoid from the Green Guide: www.thegreenguide.com/gg/pdf/dirtydozenfold3.pdf. Or, make your own natural soap: www.teachsoap.com/recipes.html.

Photo: Corbis Australia

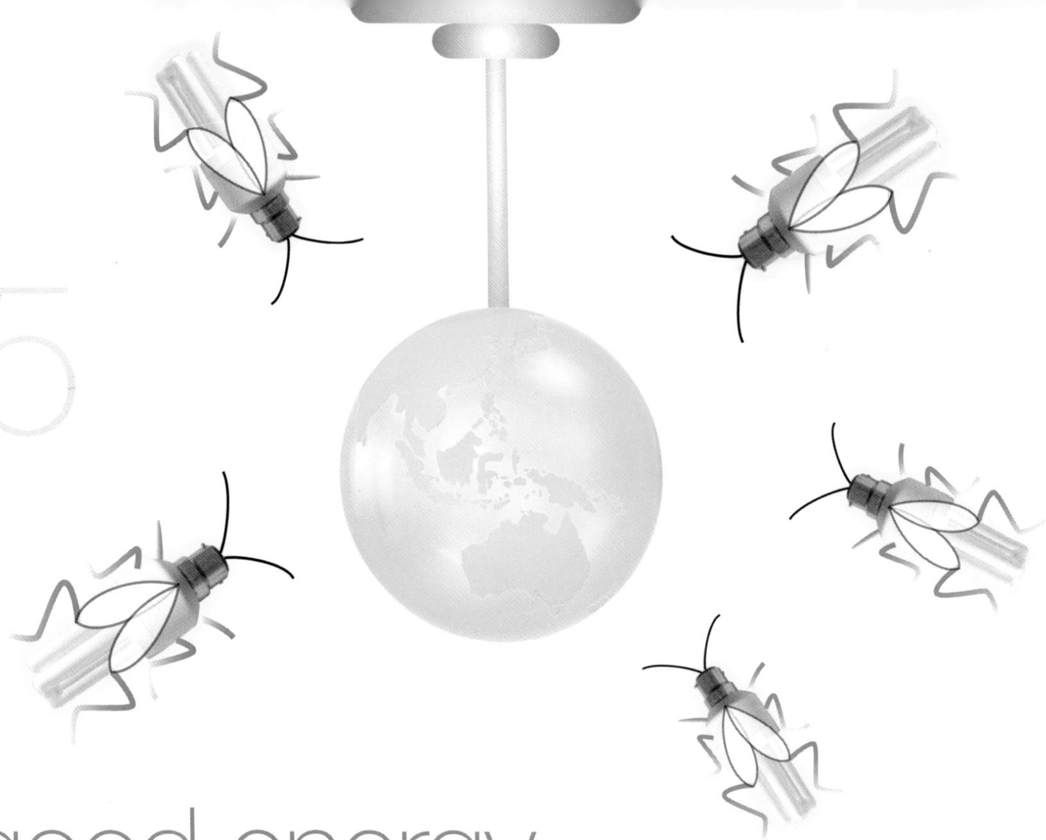

15

good energy

Compact fluorescent lights (CFLs) may look funny, but they use 65–75 percent less electricity than normal incandescent bulbs, and they last up to ten times longer. So while a CFL costs more, over its five-year lifespan it will take about $80 off the household electricity bill. More important, replacing a regular bulb with a CFL will keep about 1,430 pounds of greenhouse gases from being pumped into the atmosphere.

Fact: When you turn on an incandescent light bulb, only 10 percent of the electricity used is turned into light. The other 90 percent is wasted as heat.

Do an audit of how many bulbs still have to be changed to CFLs in your house, and share the audit with your family.

Illustration: Marian Kyte

16

lights out

It's simple to turn the light off when you leave a room—the hard part is remembering to do it! Tons of greenhouse gases can be reduced every year if lights are just turned off when they're not needed. During the day you can often just open a curtain to let in the light rather than use more electricity. Take a quick look around your home right now—how many lights are on? Are they all necessary?

Reduce greenhouse gases right away—how many unnecessary lights can you turn off in your house right now?

Illustration: Marian Kyte. Light switch photo: Olivier Le Queinec/Shutterstock

17

recycle at home

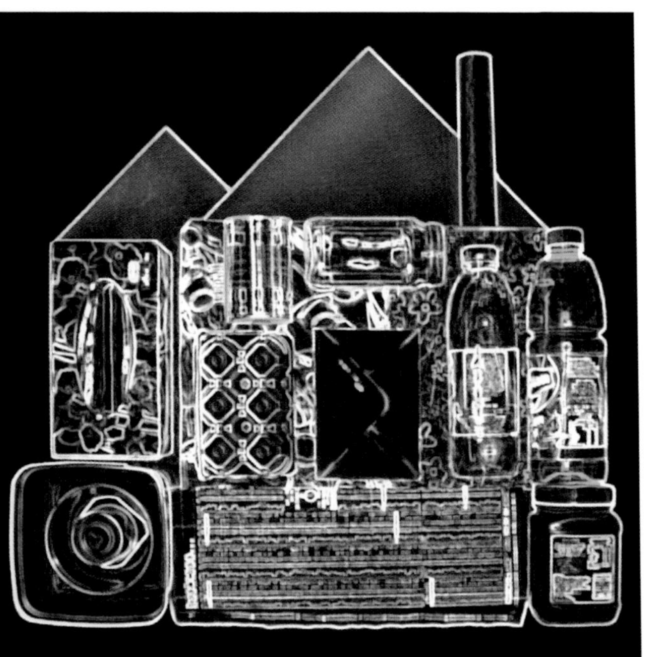

Dump it or recycle it? Recycling is so important: recycling one aluminum can uses only 5 percent of the energy needed to make a new one—and it takes more than 500 years for an aluminum can to break down! Every ton of paper that is recycled saves 17 trees, 380 gallons of oil, over 4,000 kilowatts of electricity, and more than 7,000 gallons of water…then there's glass and paper and plastic, all of which need to be recycled, too. Throwing the wrong trash in the recycling bin will make recycling useless, though, so put everything in the right container—it will make a BIG difference. Make sure our planet doesn't become one big garbage dump.

Inspect your trash every week before putting it out for collection or taking it to the dump. Make sure all your recyclables have been sorted correctly.

Illustration left: Marian Kyte and Lachlan Chang
Top: Courtesy Clean Up Australia

unplugged 18

When you walk through your house at night, how many little red and green lights can you see? All those lights—from TVs, DVD players, stereo systems, radios, and video game boxes—even in stand-by mode, cost money—about $75 a year in electricity—and that electricity creates about 190 pounds each year of greenhouse gases. So unplug your electronic devices. You do need to be careful, since some electronics will lose their programming if they are unplugged, so ask your grown-ups first.

Put power strips with individual switches in easy-to-reach places so you can turn things off easily. You'll be preventing greenhouse gases from going into the atmosphere by flicking that one switch.

Photo: Corbis Australia

19 hanging out

The washing machine is the second-biggest water guzzler in your home. No one wants to wear smelly clothes, but decide whether something could be worn again before you throw it in the dirty clothes basket. A clothesline is the clean, green alternative to the electric clothes dryer—it produces no greenhouse gases, and it's free. One load in a clothes dryer pumps about six pounds of greenhouse gas into the atmosphere. Try not to use your washing machine or clothes dryer unless you really have to.

When you come in from the rain in wet clothes, hang them up to dry—don't throw them in the dryer! On sunny days, volunteer to hang clothes outside on the clothesline. And don't throw any clothing in the hamper unless it looks dirty or smells bad.

Illustration: Marian Kyte and Lachlan Chang

20

clean and green

When you're helping with the chores, have you ever noticed that some cleaning products make you sneeze or your eyes water? It's probably because the products are full of irritating chemicals. Natural cleaning products are healthier and don't cause indoor pollution. Plain soap and water works for many jobs. Then there's vinegar, lemon juice, and baking soda to remove stains. Cheaper, better, fresher—how good is that!

You can find out how to make window cleaner and other simple, safe cleaning products. Go to www.care2.com/greenliving/make-your-own-non-toxic-cleaning-kit.html.

Super Lemon
Wow!
Sparkle!
S
See his awesome powers clean your room in a flash!

Illustration: Marian Kyte and Lachlan Chang

The great outdoors is a great place to think about all the other things that live on Earth. Everything in the universe is precious—the sun, the stars, the moon, the air, the oceans, and all the plants, animals, and insects. It is up to us to take care of it all.

outdoors

21 home-grown

The farther your food has to travel to reach your plate, the more energy is used—and that means more greenhouse gases that are going into the atmosphere. Why not grow food right in your own backyard, in pots on your balcony, or in a sunny spot in your house? You can't be more eco-efficient than that! Tomatoes, salad greens, and herbs are easy to grow, don't need much room, and can be grown indoors or out. Blueberry bushes and broccoli plants don't take up much space. You can even grow peppers and tomatoes in tubs on a balcony.

Get started on your own garden; buy some seedlings to grow in yogurt containers or egg cartons.

Photos: Marian Kyte

22

layer upon layer

Fruit and vegetable scraps, grass clippings, and leaves make up nearly 40 percent of household waste. By starting your own compost bin or worm farm, you can recycle all your green waste at home to produce a fantastic natural fertilizer that will improve your garden. In sandy soils, compost helps build soil structure, retain moisture, and provide nutrients. In heavy soils it improves drainage. A compost bin doesn't have to be smelly—you just need to find the best kind for your home. And remember, don't put any meat into the compost—it's for vegetable matter only.

Put a separate container in your kitchen for compost scraps, and learn how to make compost. Visit www.ehow.com/how_3541_begin-compost-pile.html.

Illustration: Marian Kyte

23

worm farms eat my poop?

Do you have a pet dog? Being a responsible pet owner, you always pick up the dog poop. But what do you do with it? Put it in a plastic bag and send it to a landfill, where it will sit for hundreds of years? Not a very eco-friendly solution. However, clever people are figuring out better ways to dispose of all that dog poop. San Francisco has started converting dog-doo into methane gas for fuel. And in Australia and New Zealand, worm farms are used to convert Fido's waste into great fertilizer.

Find out if your community is worm farming or composting pet waste, and if it isn't, suggest that they start. Here are three websites that show how: http://www.composters.com/vermiculture-worms/pet-poo-converter_53_4.php; http://www.wormmainea.com/projects.html; and http://www.thewormman.com/worms/home.html.

Photo: Marian Kyte

pets 24

Pets come in all shapes and sizes and can make wonderful companions. But whether your pet is a dog, a cat, a guinea pig, a rabbit, a mouse, or a fish, it comes with responsibilities. Whatever pet you decide is best for you, it will be your responsibility to make sure that your pet does not injure or kill other animals, such as native birds, that live in your area. If you have a cat or dog, it's best to keep it inside at night to protect other birds or animals.

Reuse old socks to make toys for your pets. To learn how, visit www.thefabricofourlives.com/Lifestyle/SockToysDog.

Photo: Corbis Australia

25

walking the dog

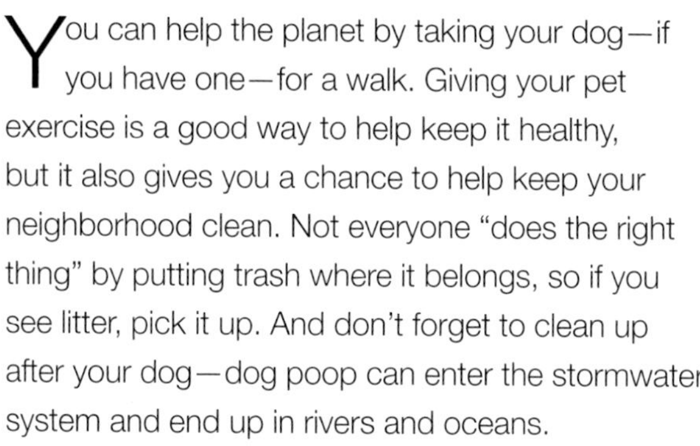

You can help the planet by taking your dog—if you have one—for a walk. Giving your pet exercise is a good way to help keep it healthy, but it also gives you a chance to help keep your neighborhood clean. Not everyone "does the right thing" by putting trash where it belongs, so if you see litter, pick it up. And don't forget to clean up after your dog—dog poop can enter the stormwater system and end up in rivers and oceans.

Take a biodegradable bag with you whenever you go for a walk with your dog, and pick up all the litter that you see.

Photo: Corbis Australia

26

feed your pets well

If you believe "you are what you eat," then what about your pets? Have you read the label on your pet's food? Is it full of chemicals and stuff you wouldn't want in your own food? You can now buy organic pet food with no additives to harm your pet or the environment. Organic pet food is high in food value, so your pet needs less of it, and it helps prevent allergies, improves behavior, and makes your pet feel better. Naturally, before you change your pet's diet, you should talk to your vet. Remember to use ceramic or metal bowls for your pet's food and water, not plastic ones. Some plastics will leach chemicals that could harm your pet.

If you use canned food or a cardboard box of dry food, recycle the container—don't just throw it in the trash.

Photo: Corbis Australia

27

diary of a bug

The natural world is full of wonders—from the mammoth whales in the oceans to the tiny bugs or amazing flowers in the garden. Why not choose your own observation spot and spend time there regularly to see what's happening? Just find a quiet area in the yard or a local park. Over a long period of time, observe the plants and creatures that live there. How do they change with the seasons? What birds visit?

Keep a diary of what you see in your observation spot. Buy some ladybugs that you can release into your garden area. Ladybugs are not only safe for you and your plants, they eat pests, so there's no need to use pesticides.

Illustration: Marian Kyte and Lachlan Chang

28

enjoy your world

The world is always changing—so keep an eye on your favorite places and watch how they change with the different seasons. Are the trees evergreens, or do they lose their leaves in winter and burst into flower in spring? Even if you live in a city, you probably have a park nearby…so wherever you live, find a place that makes you feel good, and enjoy your world. Learn to appreciate what nature is offering us.

Enjoying your world means helping to care for it…so help the planet even more by learning to protect that outdoor space. Keep it clean and unspoiled. Pick up garbage if you see it. Leave your favorite space even cleaner than you found it.

Photo: Chris Bennett

29

keep fit and healthy

If you want to help save the world, you can start with yourself. Get outside and exercise! Join a team and play a sport. Take a walk on the beach, swim, hike, ride a bike to your friend's house, go for a walk in the woods. Open up your lungs—breathe deep and smell the fresh air. Eating raw, fresh foods produced locally and without chemicals or pesticides is good for you and will help protect you from disease—and, of course, those foods are better for the planet. So by staying healthy, you can help keep our planet healthy, too!

Keep track of the time you spend indoors, and try to balance it hour-for-hour with outdoor activities. Keep a diary of the foods you eat—how many are local, fresh, and good for you?

Photos left: Corbis Australia. Top: Marian Kyte

30

heavens above!

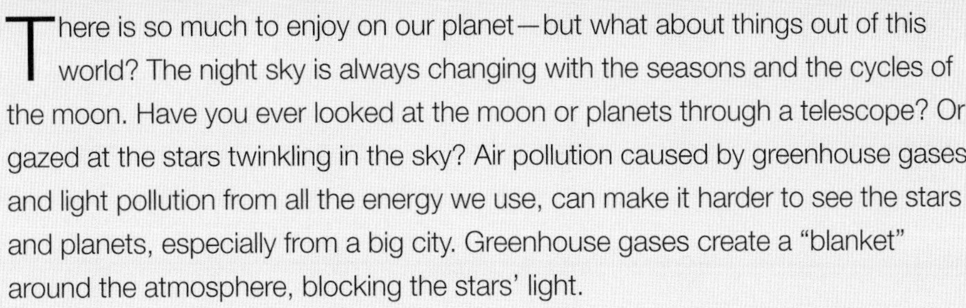

There is so much to enjoy on our planet—but what about things out of this world? The night sky is always changing with the seasons and the cycles of the moon. Have you ever looked at the moon or planets through a telescope? Or gazed at the stars twinkling in the sky? Air pollution caused by greenhouse gases, and light pollution from all the energy we use, can make it harder to see the stars and planets, especially from a big city. Greenhouse gases create a "blanket" around the atmosphere, blocking the stars' light.

Go out at night and look up at the stars—can you find the Big Dipper? Make a list of the things you use that create greenhouse gases. Then make a promise to lower your use of those things, so fewer greenhouse gases will block your view of the stars!

Moon photo: Corbis Australia

What do Cameron Diaz, Leonardo DiCaprio, Al Gore, Tim Flannery, Ian Kiernan, Coldplay, and Missy Higgins all have in common? They want us to be green. You too can be an eco-celebrity! Meet up with your friends to discuss ways to be green in your school, home, or community.

with friends

31

green celebrities

Who is your favorite celebrity? Does he or she care about the future of the planet? You can go to www.looktothestars.org/celebrity, where more than 700 celebrities are listed. There are details of the charities they support, so you can check them out for yourself. Many famous Americans, such as George Clooney, Sheryl Crow, Jake Gyllenhaal, and Alicia Keys, are actively involved in the future of the planet. Write to your favorite actor, singer, or athlete, and ask them what they are doing to help keep our planet clean and green.

Find out what your favorite star does to help the environment, and then see what you can do to join in. Maybe you can join the same environmental organizations that your celebrity supports.

32

support charities

There are so many ways we can help make the world a better place for everyone. Not only can we change our habits to save our planet's resources, we can also help our favorite charity make other people's lives better. Many charities recycle and reuse clothing, furniture, and household appliances that would otherwise be thrown away. See what you can find out about different charity organizations and what they do to help keep the Earth green. Maybe you and your friends can help them by fund-raising at school or in your community. You'll find a list of U.S. environmental charities, listed nationally and by state, at www.eco-usa.net. Another great list can be found at: www.looktothestars.org/category/13-environment.

Adopt a green charity with your friends and see what you can do to support it.

Photo: Chris Bennett

33

discuss the world

It's pretty obvious that you and your friends are going to be around longer than the adults in your life. This is YOUR planet. There is lots of information available about the environmental problems we all face and what you can do to make sure the Earth—and you!—have a future to look forward to. Find out all you can about what is happening, and talk about it at home, at school, and with your friends. Search the Web, read books and newspapers, and watch movies. It's not too late to make a difference. Remember: YOU have the power to influence others' decisions. That's why we say "Discuss the world—it matters!"

Read newspapers and watch the news to keep up-to-date with what's happening to the environment. Write a letter to your local newspaper and ask them what steps they are taking to reduce their waste and help keep the planet green. Tell them what you're doing.

Photo: Chris Bennett

34

write to politicians

Have you heard the old saying, "The pen is mightier than the sword?" If there is something you think your local town council, state government, or even the federal government isn't doing, or could do better, why not write a letter or send an email? It could be a private letter just from you, or it could be from your whole class—or even the whole school! If there are enough people interested in an issue, you could even organize a petition. To be more effective, don't just complain—make positive suggestions. But remember to keep letters short and to the point—politicians are busy people, so keep it catchy!

Write to your local town council member or mayor and ask what he or she is doing to help climate change in your town or community. Make suggestions!

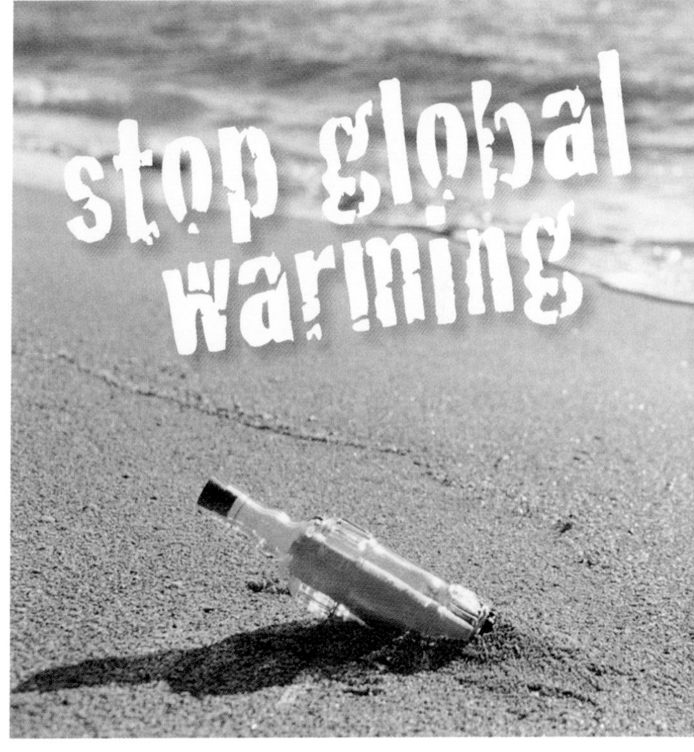

Photo: Corbis Australia

35 books with a message

If you enjoy reading, you might want to find some books about the environment. There are hundreds of books available that focus on the wonders of the natural world, the science of global warming and climate change, and ways you can help create a sustainable future. You can find an extensive list organized by theme and age range at www.childsake.com.

Give a copy of your favorite environmental book as a present to others, and include a homemade bookmark tucked into the page that contains a good suggestion for helping the environment.

Photo: Corbis Australia

seeing is believing

Al Gore's award-winning documentary *An Inconvenient Truth* has generated a lot of discussion and debate about global warming. But messages about caring for the environment can also be found in light-hearted animated features you might enjoy, such as *A Bug's Life, Antz, Finding Nemo, Over the Hedge,* and *Happy Feet.* Other movies that look at the dangers facing our planet's polar regions include *March of the Penguins* and *The White Planet.* Leonardo DiCaprio narrates *The 11th Hour,* which focuses on the warning signs of environmental disaster so vividly imagined in the movie *The Day After Tomorrow.* There are plenty more environmental films in production at the moment—keep an eye out for them.

Hold a movie afternoon with your friends or at school and raise money for your chosen environmental cause or charity.

make a movie!

Borrow a video camera and make your very own movie! You can do it alone or with a group of friends. Choose a topic with a green theme that interests you or relates to something that's important to your family or local area. You can have fun researching and writing the script, taking photographs, creating a storyboard, and making props and costumes—just remember to keep it short and catchy. Once the film's finished, you can organize a showing to raise money for your school or favorite green charity.

Investigate competitions for short movies, and enter your green movie to help share your environmental message.

Photo: Marian Kyte

be inspired 38

Another way of appreciating the world with your friends is to enjoy art inspired by the environment, or art that is actually a part of the environment. Most cities have outdoor art shows, and most towns have public artworks in parks or on main streets. Do you have a favorite piece of public artwork that highlights the environment? Do you have an idea for a piece of art you would like to see in your environment—a sculpture, a mural, a graffiti wall? If you do, you could ask your teacher to help you create it, or approach your local town council, which may have funds available for outdoor art, particularly if it draws attention to how we need to change the way we live to save the planet.

Seek permission to create a mural inspired by nature, at school or in your local community. If you can't use an outside wall, create a mural on a long strip of butcher's paper and attach it to your classroom wall, a wall in the assembly hall at school, or the local community center.

Photo: Tom Millner & Adam Proctor "Cultivating Crabs," recycled farm parts.
Photo: Jack Bett, *Sculpture by the Sea*, Bondi, 2004.

39

swap club

How many books and DVDs do you really need to own? It's nice to have them on a shelf to look at, but you'll probably only read or watch them once or twice. Joining the local library or video store means you can borrow rather than buy. Set up a trading club with your friends to share CDs and computer games. Aside from the money you save, you'll also be helping the environment because making, packaging, transporting, and getting rid of everything you buy involves energy, water, and waste.

Fact: CDs are made from polycarbonate and acrylic plastic and are covered with a layer of aluminum. This makes them very difficult to break down and recycle, so when you can, download music and movies and store them on hard drives that can be reused.

 **Set up a regular trading club with your friends.**

Illustration: Marian Kyte

40 true green party

Next time you organize a birthday party—or any kind of celebration—why not make it green? What makes a great party? Food, decorations, fancy clothes, presents, wrapping paper, and cards. But what happens afterward? Most of that stuff just gets thrown away. You can still have a great party and not add to the Earth's pollution problem. Use recycled materials for costumes, decorations, and wrapping paper. Provide locally grown organic food, and serve "nibbles" on one big platter rather than lots of smaller, disposable plates. Let people know that it's a green party when you invite them.

Fact: Fifteen trees must be cut down to make each ton of the glossy paper that is used in cards, magazines, and catalogs.

Make invitations out of recycled materials for your next party—or, better still, send an e-invite.

Photo: Corbis Australia

Every year, the average American family produces 3.3 tons of landfill waste—enough to fill a 3-bedroom house. Imagine how it would help the environment if we all chose to reuse things we have and to buy recycled products instead of filling up our garbage dumps with things we don't need. Think twice before you buy something. Remember: Less is more.

buying stuff

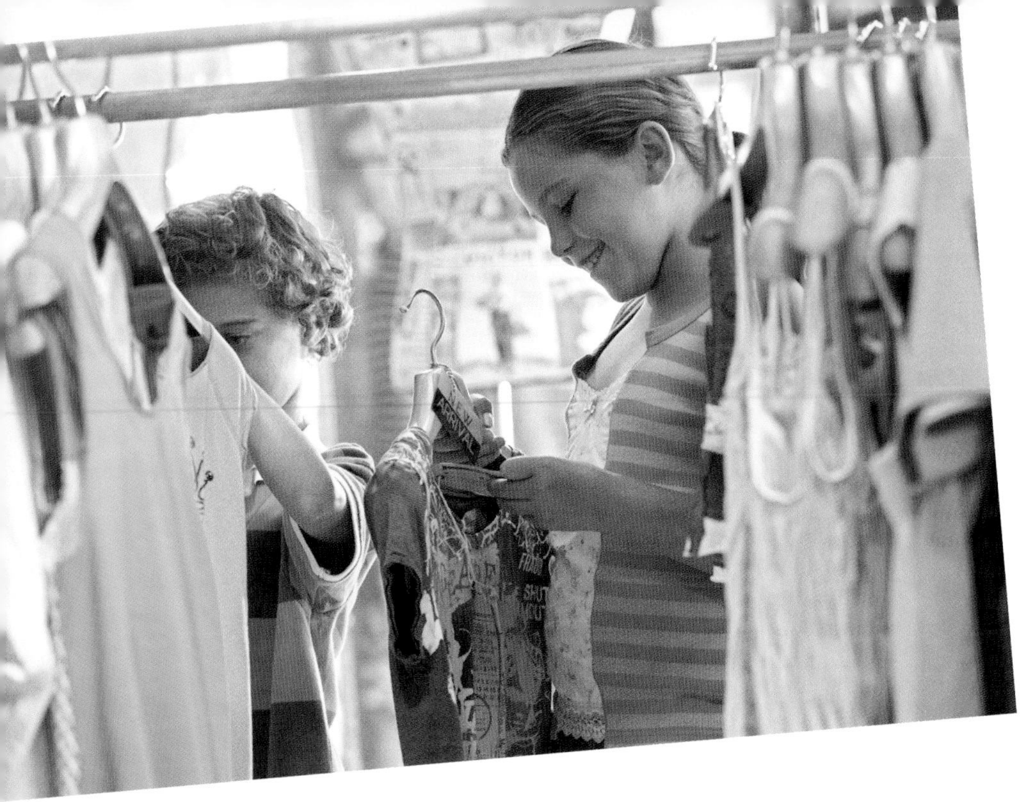

41

do you really need it?

Not everyone lives in a consumer society—think of people in poorer countries who don't have much and who reuse or recycle nearly everything. Why do we always want more things? Every day we see or read things that tell us to buy the newest, the latest, the biggest, the best. Now that you know how much stuff is thrown away, you can see that one way of helping the environment is to not buy so much new stuff in the first place! Ask yourself if you *really* need it. Just remember: You are who you *are,* not what you *have.*

Go online and find out about the global movement called "The Compact," started by people in San Francisco, which aims to reduce unnecessary consumption.

42

don't believe the hype

Do you believe everything you're told in advertising? Will eating fast food or drinking a particular soft drink make you smarter, wiser, richer, or a better person? Advertisers simply want you to buy their products—but you are smarter than that! You know that the more stuff you buy, the more the Earth's resources are used up. So think carefully about what you buy, and be aware of what it's made of. Buy products that will last or can be recycled—or ask, "Can I make this myself?"

When you see an ad, make a game of it—come up with a reason why you don't need the product! You may be surprised at how often you realize you can easily live without it!

Illustration: Marian Kyte

43 just add imagination

It doesn't take much imagination to see how you can make some great things from what is usually thrown out. Some cities, and many community centers, have places where you can get an amazing range of useful reusable and recycled materials. Not only do they have things you can use to make funky art, but they have recycled building materials as well. If there isn't such a place near where you live, you can now buy an amazing range of recycled and reusable items online. Of course, you don't have to buy garbage—just take a look at what people throw away during clean-ups and leave at the dump. There's so much that can be turned into useful, attractive, and fun objects.

Check out www.planetpals.com for crafts that can be made with recycled materials.

Illustration: Marian Kyte

44

fresh is best

Fresh fruits and vegetables are not only good for you—they're good for the planet because greenhouse gases are not created in processing, canning, freezing, or packaging. Make your own food instead of buying pre-made food. You can find recipes on the Web or buy a second-hand cookbook. Cooking is more fun than opening a package. And you can control what goes into what you make—use organic and natural ingredients and give chemicals the "heave-ho."

Once you've figured out what you can cook easily, invite some friends over and impress them with an eco-meal, or prepare an eco-meal for your family. Start by making a fresh fruit salad—and you're on your way! You can find some great recipes at http://holidays.kaboose.com/earth-day/earth-day-recipes.html

Photo: Corbis Australia. Details: Marian Kyte.

45

what's in it?

Everything you buy should have a label on it that tells you what's in it, how to care for it, and where it was made. Understanding this information gives you a better idea of the impact that product has on the Earth's resources. Is the fabric natural or synthetic? Does the product carry a Fair Trade label to show that workers have been paid a fair wage to produce it? If the farmers get a fair price for their crop, they will be better able to take care of their land and create a more sustainable community, which is better for the planet. Is the product made locally or far away? These are just some of the things you can learn from labels.

Next time you go shopping with your family, see how green you can be. Check the labels of the things you are buying, and try to buy items that are naturally grown, organic, or locally grown.

Photo: Corbis Australia

46 packaging pileup

How much do you weigh? 80 pounds? 110? Well, every person in America sends a whopping 259 pounds of packaging to landfills every year! The average in Europe is about 132 pounds, with the best recyclers achieving figures as low as 66 pounds per person. So come on America, we have to do better! Currently we recycle about 59 percent of our packaging. If we could boost that to 65 percent, we would keep more than 2 million tons of packaging from going into landfills each year. It won't happen overnight, but you can make a start by not buying things in useless packaging. If enough people do this, maybe the message will get back to the manufacturers.

Fact: Every year 13 billion steel cans (food cans, drink cans, and so on) are produced. Only about a quarter of the steel used has been recycled.

When you buy something that has unnecessary packaging, send a message to the retailer by leaving the excess packaging behind at the store! And always check for the recycling symbol on plastic packaging—recycle everything you can.

Photo: Marian Kyte

47

support the locals

The farther food travels from where it's grown to where it's sold, the more greenhouse gases are pumped into the atmosphere through the gasoline and diesel fumes given off by trucks, trains, and planes as they transport the food. The same goes for the distance you travel to buy the food. So shop locally. If possible convince your family to take reusable shopping bags and walk, or ride your bikes, to nearby shops a few times a week. You'll be getting exercise while keeping the atmosphere cleaner. If your only nearby grocery store is a large, national chain, you can still make a difference—choose foods that are produced locally over food produced far away.

Find your nearest farmers' market selling fresh, locally grown fruit and veggies, and shop there as often as you can (remember to bring reusable shopping bags!).

Photo: Marian Kyte. Courtesy Arthur's Bavarian Bakehouse.

48

buying green

Organic food is grown without the use of artificial fertilizers and pesticides or genetic modification. The farmer works with nature rather than against it by recycling natural materials to maintain soil fertility and encouraging natural methods of pest and disease control. Not only does organic food contain higher concentrations of vitamins and minerals—it usually tastes better as well. You can also buy an amazing range of clothing, footwear, and accessories made from organically grown fibers.

How many items in your local supermarket or clothing store can you find that are labeled "organic" or made with organic fibers? For healthier, greener living, ask your mom and dad to buy organic.

Illustration: Marian Kyte

49

just say no...

SAY NO TO PLASTIC BAGS

Did you know Americans use more than 277 million plastic bags a day? That means we use more than 100 BILLION bags each year, or 330 plastic bags for every adult and child. That's equal to dumping 12 million barrels of oil each year! And, sadly, we only recycle about 2 percent of those bags. Some U.S. towns have started banning the use of plastic bags in stores, and places like Whole Foods are no longer providing them to customers. You can understand why when you realize that they last up to 1,000 years in landfills, and millions end up as garbage that kills wildlife on land and in the ocean, lakes, and rivers. Take a reusable bag when you go shopping, and say "no" to the plastic bags the store offers you.

Encourage your grown-ups to keep reusable bags in the trunk of the family car to make sure you have them when you go shopping, and bring your own reusable bags whenever you run errands. Join the "Bring Your Own Bag" movement!

Photo: Glen Jones/iStock

Photo: David Schrader/iStock

50 buy american

Just as buying from local markets is good for your community, so is buying products that are grown or made in the United States. Transporting products by plane or ship from overseas means more greenhouse gases are created, because carbon dioxide fumes come from the planes and ships in transit. So buying American-made products is not just good for our economy—creating jobs and improving our living standards—it's also good for the atmosphere. Things made overseas might be cheaper, but there's an environmental cost to consider.

Look for the words "Made in America" or "Made in the U.S.A." on labels when you go shopping, and encourage your family and friends to "buy American!"

School is the perfect place to practice the four Rs: reduce, reuse, recycle, rethink. Just as you can make a difference at home, you and your classmates can work together to make a difference at school by being water-wise, energy efficient, and creative.

at school

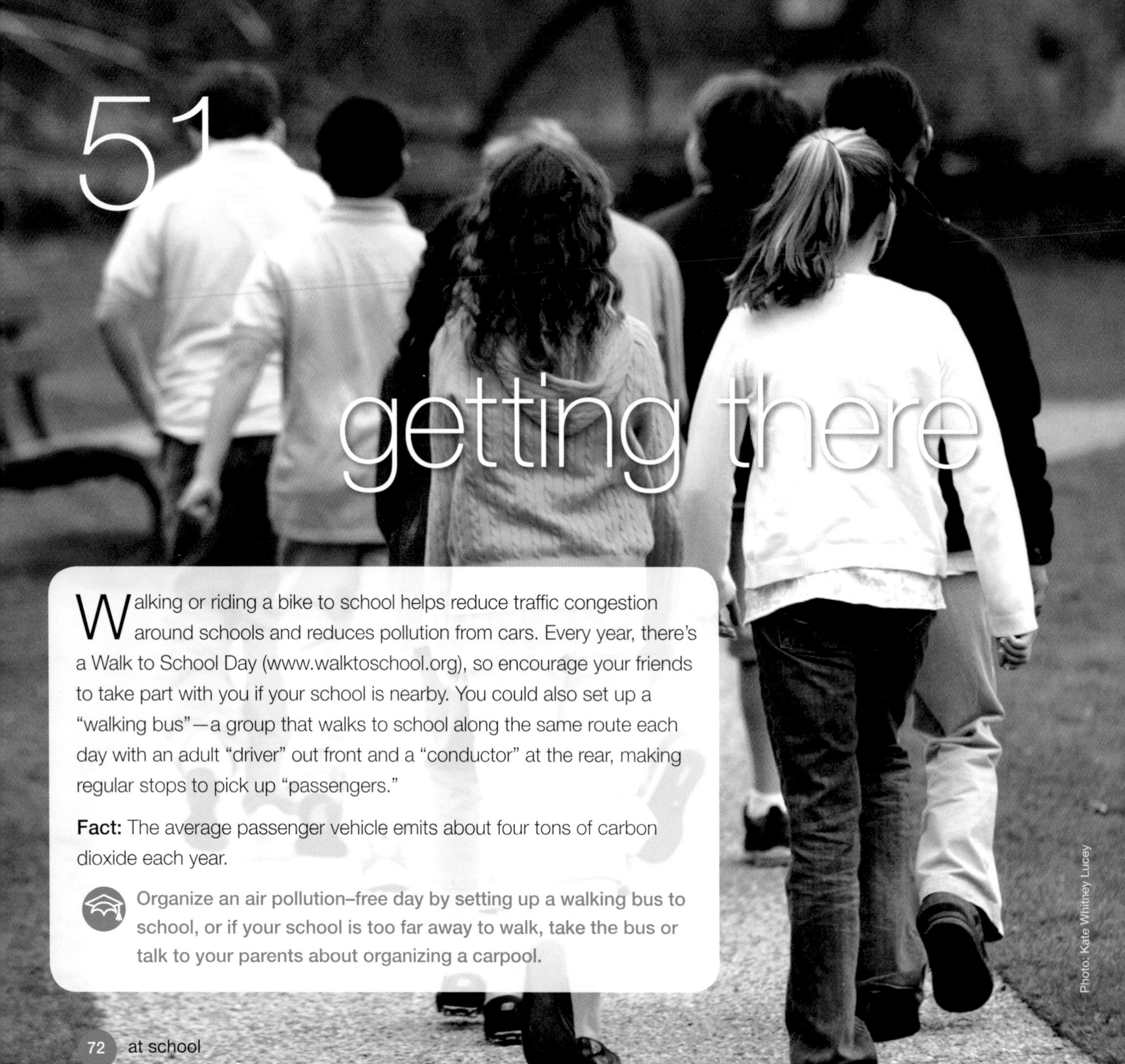

51 getting there

Walking or riding a bike to school helps reduce traffic congestion around schools and reduces pollution from cars. Every year, there's a Walk to School Day (www.walktoschool.org), so encourage your friends to take part with you if your school is nearby. You could also set up a "walking bus"—a group that walks to school along the same route each day with an adult "driver" out front and a "conductor" at the rear, making regular stops to pick up "passengers."

Fact: The average passenger vehicle emits about four tons of carbon dioxide each year.

Organize an air pollution–free day by setting up a walking bus to school, or if your school is too far away to walk, take the bus or talk to your parents about organizing a carpool.

Photo: Kate Whitney Lucey

52

the four Rs

reduce, reuse, recycle, rethink

Being at school presents another great opportunity to practice the "four Rs."
REDUCE what you use and what you throw away—such as plastic bags;
REUSE as much as you can—print on both sides of paper, for example;
RECYCLE everything that can be recycled—paper, glass, cans, and plastic;
RETHINK how you use things—switch off computers and lights.
These are just a few simple examples of how YOU can make a difference.

With your teacher's help, make a list of all the ways your class can reduce, reuse, recycle, and rethink to help the environment.

Photo: Corbis Australia

53 recycle paper

When computers first began to be widely used, people said they would soon replace paper, and talked about "the paperless office." But today we throw away more paper than anything else. Everyone can make a difference, so whenever you have to do some photocopying, use both sides of the paper—you'll cut your paper use in half. Writing on both sides of every sheet of paper and cutting up scrap paper for artwork or to make notepads are other ways you can use paper more efficiently. And do you recycle the paper that you use? Make sure you have a recycling bin in your classroom!

Fact: Americans use an average of 700 pounds of paper products per person each year.

It takes 17 trees to produce 1 ton of paper. Figure out how many trees you could save in a year by reusing and recycling your classroom paper.

Illustration: Marian Kyte

pens, pencils, and ...

54

Would you believe that more than 2 billion pens are produced in the USA every year? Most are thrown away when they're empty; in America, we are tossing 1.5 billion ballpoint pens into landfills every year. You can do your part to reduce that waste by buying refillable pens—there are even refillable felt-tip pens now. Look for pencils that are made out of wood from specially planted forests, recycled paper, old plastic cups, corn starch, or wood chips.

Look for school supplies made from recycled materials. In addition to pens and pencils, there are recycled scissors, paper clips, Post-it notes, rulers, and more. And ask your teacher to purchase recycled classroom supplies, too.

Session 1: Paper Audit

Task: Brainstorm as a class different types of paper used in the school.

Papers used for writing on
And painting pictures too
Papers used in photocopiers
Even in the bathroom!
Reduce, re-use, recycle and re-think
Save our trees today!

eat your packaging

55

What makes the most waste—a chocolate bar or a fresh apple? Unlike candy bars that need to be wrapped, most fruits and vegetables come in their very own "packaging," provided by Mother Nature. Producing fresh fruit, vegetables, and nuts requires less energy and water than making processed foods, so eating more raw food is better for the environment. As a bonus, fresh raw fruits and vegetables can help protect you against health problems such as obesity, heart disease, and cancer. So pack fresh fruits and veggies in your lunch bag—and don't forget to put leftovers in the compost bin or worm farm.

Plan a menu of your class's favorite foods that need no packaging.

Photo: Chris Bennett

lunchtime

Do you take your lunch to school every day? It's cheaper than buying it and produces less waste than getting it from the school cafeteria. Instead of buying a new plastic lunch box to take it in, reuse a take-out container—they are just as good. You can also reuse bread wrappers and plastic packaging. There are many ways you can help cut down on waste and reduce the amount of litter in your schoolyard. Does your school have a "green canteen" or vending area that serves healthy, sustainable food products? If not, who can you talk to to start one?

Fact: Washing your bottles and cartons before recycling them saves the energy it would take to clean them at the recycling plant.

Help organize a trash-free lunch day at school, and make it a regular, fun thing to do.

Photos, upper: Stockbyte/Getty Images and Chris Bennett.
Photo, lower: Kate Whitney Lucey

57

BYO water bottle

Taking a bottle of water to school is good for your health. But buying bottled water is bad for the health of the planet. If the water has to be transported by truck or plane, that means more carbon emissions go into the Earth's atmosphere. Then more emissions result from producing the bottle. Even recycling the bottle uses energy. Americans go through 2.5 million plastic water bottles every hour, and 30 million end up in landfills each year. American cities have good-quality tap water, and many people have simple filter systems at home. So refill an environmentally friendly water bottle from the faucet and take that to school. Why pay more for something you can get for pennies straight from your faucet at home and school?

The next time you go shopping, ask your grown-up to buy you an eco-friendly water bottle that you can refill every day and take to school.

Photo: Kate Whitney Lucey

every drop is precious 58

be water-wise

Every drop of water is precious. When you use the bathroom at school (and at home), you can save water by being water-wise. Be sure to turn off the tap as soon as you have washed your hands. Report leaking faucets and toilet bowls because a dripping faucet can waste up to eight gallons of water a week—about as much as you'd use to take one shower. You can be water-wise in the classroom as well—wash paintbrushes in a bucket and not under a running tap.

Be a water monitor at school—keep an eye on faucets and toilets, and report all leaks as you notice them.

Illustration: Lachlan Chang

59

every drop counts

More than 70 percent of the Earth's surface is covered by water, but 97 percent of it is saltwater in the oceans, and 2 percent is freshwater trapped in the polar ice caps. This leaves just 1 percent for us to use. So you can see just what a precious resource water is. This is especially true if you live in a dry or warm part of the country. How is water managed at your school? Do you have tanks to catch rainwater? Is waste water recycled for use on school lawns and gardens?

Talk to your teacher about participating in the United Nations–designated World Water Day in March each year. There are lots of activities your class can do to remind others that water is precious. To learn more, check out http://www.worldwaterday.org/.

Photo: Kate Whitney Lucey

60

bright ideas

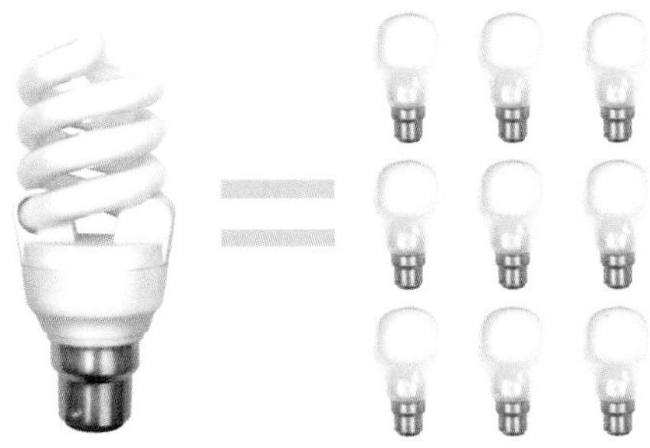

You've already learned a lot of ways you can help save the planet AND save money at the same time. Whatever you do at home, you can also do at school. So if you see lights and appliances left on, either turn them off or find out who is responsible and remind them. And what about those lights? Are they eco-friendly compact fluorescent bulbs or energy-guzzling incandescents? If you think your school is not doing the right thing, speak to an adult and find out ways to make changes. Remember—the future of the world is in your hands.

Think twice before you turn on a heater or air conditioner. Make a sign and post it in your classroom to remind everyone to do the same.

Illustration: Marian Kyte

Working together with your friends at school will help to make environmental change a reality. Learn how to calculate your school's carbon footprint, and then find out how to reduce it. It's all about teamwork!

teamwork

61

hands up for Earth Day!

There are many environmental events and activities throughout the year. One big one is Earth Day, a worldwide event on April 22. It started in 1970 with 20 million Americans, and in 2008 1 billion people from 184 countries around the world took part. There is also Clean Up the World, held every September, which involves millions of volunteers in more than 120 countries. And there's Earth Hour, which took place for the second year in April 2008. People in countries and cities around the world turned off all their lights for 1 hour to raise awareness of the need to reduce coal-produced electricity, the greatest contributor to global warming.

Make a calendar of all environmental events. Post it at school and home, and get friends and family to participate!

Eco Events Calendar
JANUARY
National Radon Action Month
FEBRUARY
World Wetlands Day
MARCH
Earth Hour, World Water Day
APRIL
Earth Day
Arbor Day
MAY
Clean Air Month
Fair Trade Week
JUNE
World Ocean Day
World Environment Day
JULY
National Parks & Recreation Day
AUGUST
World Indigenous Peoples Day
SEPTEMBER
Clean Up The World Day
OCTOBER
World Habitat Day
NOVEMBER
America Recycles Day & Buy Nothing Day
DECEMBER
International Volunteer Day

Photo: Courtesy of Clean Up Austtralia

think native

62

Find out which plants are native to your area (your local nurseries or gardening centers should be able to help), and start planting. Native plants attract butterflies and birdlife that will make your schoolyard a more interesting and attractive place, as well as insects that are beneficial to the school's plants and shrubs. Planting large trees helps offset the carbon dioxide your school produces. Not only that, but the trees provide shade for the playground and can help to keep buildings cool in warm months—which means less energy will be used on air-conditioning or fans.

Create a frog pond at your school. Frogs are a good indicator of the health of a natural environment. To learn how to make a frog pond, visit: http://www.frogsvilleusa.com/how-to/frog-pond.html.

Photo: Kate Whitney Lucey

63

edible garden

If you live in a warm climate, it's really fun to set up an edible garden. With your teacher and classmates, select things that you can grow during school months—vegetables such as lettuce, radishes, and tomatoes; herbs like parsley and mint; and even fruit. Keep the weeds out—they're water thieves. If you live in a cool climate, plant seeds in pots, put them in a sunny spot in your classroom, and grow your edible garden inside!

Prepare some snacks with the food you've grown in your garden and share it with the rest of the school. Show others how easy it is to be eco-friendly by growing your own fruits and veggies!

Photo: Getty Images

64

feed your garden

All schools produce a lot of food and yard waste. Setting up a school compost pile can turn this waste into excellent fertilizer for a school gardening project. Or you could set up a worm farm in your classroom. It doesn't take long for the worms to reduce food scraps, paper, and dirt to a pile of castings and liquid (it's really worm pee!). Make sure you keep the worm farm moist at all times and don't feed worms onions, garlic, or citrus scraps—they are too acidic, and your worms will leave the farm!

Fact: Almost half of the garbage we throw out every day can be turned into compost.

Here are two cool websites that tell you how to make a worm farm: http://pbskids.org/dragonflytv/show/wormfarm.html and http://www.css.cornell.edu/compost/worms/basics.html

Which team will win the worm race?
Watch out for citrus scraps!

65

carbon footprint

power **water** **travel** **waste**

Your carbon footprint is a measure of the amount of greenhouse gases you produce. You can calculate your family's carbon footprint, and so can your classmates. Find out the amount of electricity or gas your family uses each year and how many miles the family car(s) travels. Then go to www.zerofootprintkids.com or www.carboncounter.org and enter the information. Compare results with your classmates. Once you know how big your family's footprint is, you can start to figure out ways to reduce it.

Set up an eco-page on your school's website to report on the progress your class is making in reducing your families' carbon footprints, and challenge other classrooms to do the same.

66

Photo: Marian Kyte

energy use

Here's another good way you can help your school and the planet. Suggest a class project to do an energy audit of your school. Think about all the different ways energy and resources are used. Count all the light bulbs, outlets, computers, appliances, and anything else that uses electricity. Be sure to include water use—how many toilets there are, how often gardens are watered, etc. Once you have made a list, you can use it to calculate the carbon footprint of your school and come up with a checklist of how things can be improved. Repeat the audit in six months, and see if there have been any changes.

Write an article about your classroom's energy audit for your school paper or local town paper, and invite other schools to take the steps to reduce their energy use.

get creative

SAVE THE REEF!

Help stop global warming: reduce, recycle, re-use

67

Pick a green topic such as, "Say no to plastic bags," "How to recycle," or "Save water," and ask your teacher to organize a competition to see who can create the best poster to promote it. Some of your local businesses might be happy to donate prizes or to display the winning entries in their store windows. Scan in the winners' posters and print them as a calendar to sell to raise funds for other school eco-projects or for your classroom's favorite green charity.

Contact your local newspaper and ask if they would be interested in publishing photos and a story about the competition, the best posters, and how your school is trying to raise awareness of the environment.

Illustration: Lachlan Chang

68

be dramatic!

Get together with a group of friends and present your own play about the environment. Choose a topic you like—it could be about rain forests, recycling, saving water, or caring for the natural environment. Will it be a comedy, a tragedy, or a tense family drama? Brainstorm ideas for the story. You might need to choose a writer and a director, but you can all help create props and costumes out of recycled materials. This could even become a school-wide drama festival with a green theme. Promote your play in your local newspaper.

Sell tickets to your play, and donate all ticket sales to a green charity.

Illustration: Marian Kyte

Eco Festival
* celebrity speakers * food * stalls
* music * art * drama * dancing

Does your school have a special environment week as a focus for your green activities? If not, create one! You can invite guest speakers from environmental groups, community members, local celebrities, and representatives of local goverment to come and talk to students and parents; present a festival with drama, music, and visual arts, all related to the environment; have booths that sell the results of your worm farm (bottled worm pee fertilizer and bags of compost) or products from your edible garden; have a swap club to exchange clothes, games, DVDs, books, and comics; and give demonstrations of the positive things your school is doing for the environment.

Put up posters and write articles for your local and school papers to promote your environment week, invite the community, and sell tickets to raise funds for a special local environmental organization.

Illustration: Marian Kyte

70

the green team

Now that you've found out about so many things you can do at school to help save the planet, what's next? You and your friends can make all kinds of decisions and plans, but how can you be sure something will happen? Find out if your school has an environmental education policy and, if it does, how it works. If your school does not have such a policy, do some research to find out how you can help create one. Your input is important, and maybe you could join your school's environment management committee or be involved in some other way. Getting your parents involved in the local school board's environmental activities is a good way to find out what is being done at your local schools to change your world.

Find out if there are any local environmental award competitions that your school could enter, and if there are, take the lead and enter your school.

Photo: Kate Whitney Lucey

Vacations are a great excuse to visit places of wonder and excitement. Nature offers some of the best vacation ideas: snorkeling, trekking, sailing, climbing, camping, and discovering new animals, plants, and people. But going on vacation doesn't have to mean taking a break from being true green!

on vacation

71 be aware

We all love going on vacation. The challenge is to make sure we don't cause damage to the habitats of endangered plants and animals. We know the negative impact humans can have on the health of our planet, but fortunately there are ways to enjoy vacations without harming the environment. There are now specially designed vacation resorts, farm stays, and eco-tours that are guaranteed to be ecologically sustainable. One of the main organizations promoting eco-friendly tourism is the Nature Conservancy (http://www.nature.org/aboutus/travel/ecotourism/). Why not check out your favorite vacation destination and see if it is eco-aware, or if there are eco-tours available in the area?

Help your family plan your next vacation to be eco-friendly.

Photos top: Lady Elliot Island, Tourism Queensland
Below: Surfers Paradise, Tourism Queensland

72

wet and wild

The United States enjoys thousands of miles of coastline, so you may be able to see a variety of fish, whales, dolphins, and even manatees. Dolphins, in particular, are friendly and intelligent mammals—they have been much-loved by humans for centuries. Unfortunately, both manatees and dolphins are facing many problems of survival, so be aware of how to treat them properly. Whale- and dolphin-watching trips are a good way to learn more about marine life, or watch for migrating whales from high points on the East and West coasts from June to November. Aquariums are good places to learn about sea creatures and their importance to the well-being of the planet.

Make a list of three types of marine life that are in danger because of global warming and ocean pollution. Then list three things you can do that will help prevent global warming and will keep our oceans less polluted and safer for that marine life.

Photo: Monkey Mia, courtesy Tourism Western Australia

73

world heritage sites

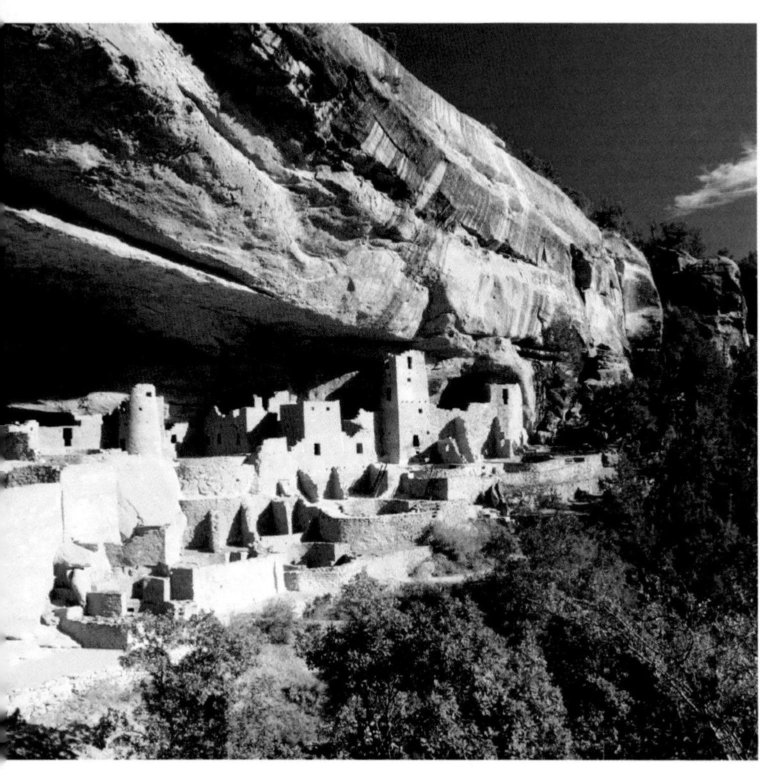

Some places are so important that they are put on the list of world heritage sites—places important to preserve because they are part of what we hand down from one generation to another. One world heritage site is the Grand Canyon, considered one of the seven natural wonders of the world. It offers spectacular views and colorful landscapes and is home to seven major ecosystems! There are many other world heritage sites in the United States, including Redwood National Park with its giant Sequoia trees, and Mesa Verde National Park with its hundreds of ancient Pueblo Indian cliff dwellings.

Learn how you can join the Junior Ranger Program and help protect world heritage sites at: http://www.nps.gov/learn/juniorranger.htm.

Photo: Duncan Gilbert/Shutterstock

74

the everglades

One of our country's most ecologically diverse and environmentally important areas is Everglades National Park. An enormous wetlands wilderness, it is home to many rare and endangered species, including panthers, manatees, and crocodiles. It's an incredible place to visit. Just be aware that this ecosystem is very fragile, so do everything you can to minimize your impact.

Fact: The Everglades used to extend from Central Florida down to Florida Bay. Now only 25 percent of the historic Everglades are left, and entire populations of birds have disappeared.

Learn more about the Everglades and how you can help save them at: http://www.nps.gov/ever/forkids/beajuniorranger.htm.

75

national parks

The original inhabitants of North America lived in harmony with the land for thousands of years. Many still do, and it is a privilege to be allowed to experience the power of this great country with them. If you visit a national park, it is essential you take great care not to pollute or damage the land. As Chief Seattle, leader of the Duwamish and Suquamish nations of the Northwest said, "The Earth does not belong to man, Man belongs to the Earth," and "Take only memories; leave nothing but footprints."

List ways visitors can treat our national parks with respect. Then write letters to the editors of your local and school newspapers offering your list as advice for anyone visiting a national park.

Photo. upper: iStock. Lower, Jason Alan/iStock

precious places

76

Visiting national parks can teach us about the natural environment and why it is important to take care of it. Canyon De Chelly holds the ancient ruins, drawings, and cliff dwellings of the Anasazi. Navajo people still live there and farm the land as their ancestors did. Alaskan natives live in many beautiful and unspoiled parts of their state, with coastline, wilderness, and a wide variety of animals. No matter where you live, how you treat the Earth affects the land and wildlife elsewhere—even far away. We must live in harmony with the land, as American Indians have for thousands of years.

Who were the original inhabitants of your area, and how did they care for the land? Can you learn ways to care for your environment from what you discover about the people who first lived there?

Photo: Karla Caspari/Shutterstock

hold the tuna!

77

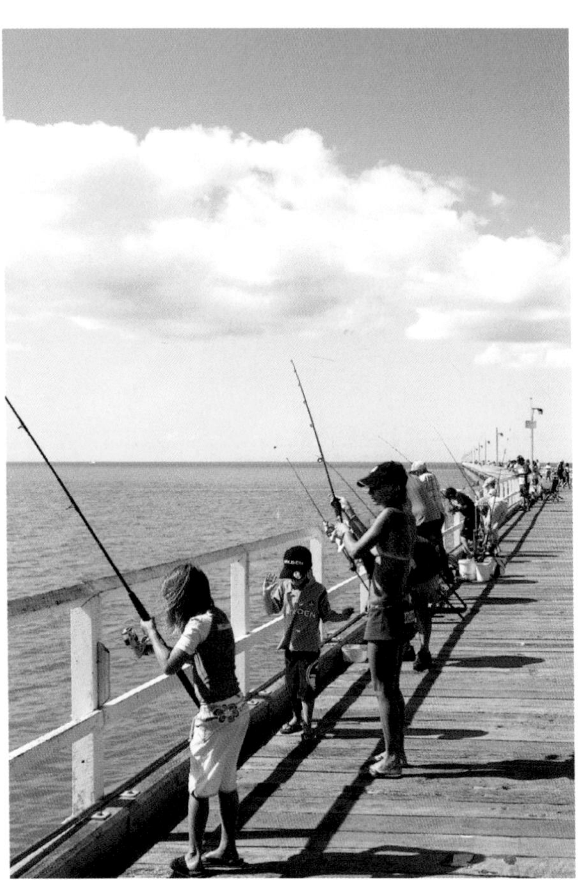

When you go on vacation to the beach, do you like to go fishing? It's a favorite pastime for many people, and eating fish is an important part of a healthy diet. Not only is it a rich source of protein, but the oils found in fish are great for your brain and heart. But many fish are seriously endangered. So whether you go fishing or buy fish from a store, make sure you don't eat species that are under threat.

Learn what fish are endangered at: http://www.montereybayaquarium.org/cr/seafoodwatch.asp or http://www.edf.org/page.cfm?tagID=1521. Put the list of endangered fish on your refrigerator to remind you what fish should be off limits.

Photo: Hervey Bay, Tourism Queensland

leave nothing but footprints

78

You don't want your own environment covered in trash, so be careful not to leave anything behind when you visit our natural wonders. If you're camping, think about how to use water for washing and keeping clean without damaging the environment. If no toilets or port-a-johns are provided, make sure you use a spot at least 100 yards from campsites and also from rivers and creeks—and bury everything at least 6 inches deep. Don't disturb the local plants and animals (or feed them), stick to paths to the beach, and don't write graffiti on or deface anything. Respect the world around you.

When you go camping, pack environmentally friendly equipment... and take every piece of litter with you when you leave.

Photo: Boulia, Tourism Queensland

79

are we there yet?

While flying can be fun, it produces large amounts of CO_2 emissions. In fact, traveling by plane is about the worst method of travel for the environment. So for your next trip, talk to your parents about taking the train, driving—or better still, taking a bus. It's a lot less stressful, is far less damaging to the air we breathe, and you get to see more of the countryside. A family of 4 flying round-trip from Boston to Disney World is responsible for an incredible 5,525 pounds of greenhouse gases in plane travel alone! And because planes release their emissions high in the atmosphere, the greenhouse effect is 3 times greater than on the ground. By comparison, that same family taking a commercial bus line would be responsible for only 1,274 pounds of CO_2.

Before your next vacation, figure out the amount of greenhouse gases you'd create by flying. Go to http://www.terrapass.com/flight/flightcalc.php.

Photo left: Losevsky Pavel/Shutterstock
Top: Judson Abts/Shutterstock

80 take off

Sometimes there is no alternative to air travel—it's a long way to swim from Chicago to Hawaii! But we can do something positive to balance the negative effect of CO_2 emissions. It's called "carbon offset." If we calculate the amount of CO_2 released by our journey, we can pay a little extra to support an industry that saves the same amount of CO_2. The money goes to planting new forests in places like Africa and Australia, or is invested in companies, such as wind farms, that produce non-polluting energy. So the next time you have to travel by plane, ask your family to offset the CO_2 released by your travel.

Visit www.terrapass.com or www.carbonfund.org to learn more about how you can offset the CO_2 released by your travel and daily activities.

Photo: Kakadu National Park (photographer unknown)

Imagine a world with no toys, no television, and no computer games. What on earth would you do? Make your own fun, that's what! You can create arts and crafts, or make presents, musical instruments, or a garden. You are limited only by your imagination.

fun things to make

81

find and seek

Have you ever wandered along a beach or city street, or through a forest, a farm, or even your own backyard, and noticed the number of different colors and textures in everything you see? Some modern artists use materials that we might think of as garbage to make works of art. You'll find amazing stuff washed up on the beach, especially after storms. And you can collect a whole range of different objects from almost anywhere and create your own art. Use old cans and bottles, or even flip-flops, like in this "Thong Bottle" made by environmental artist John Dahlsen!

See what you can collect that you can use to make art. You'll be cleaning up your environment, having fun, and making artwork—all at the same time!

Photo: "*Absolut Dahlsen*" by John Dahlsen, recycled thongs, metal and fibreglass, 4.2 m high x 1.5 m wide, 2004.

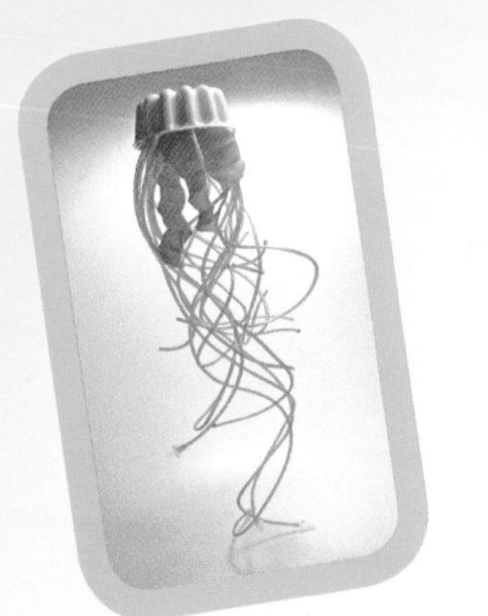

82

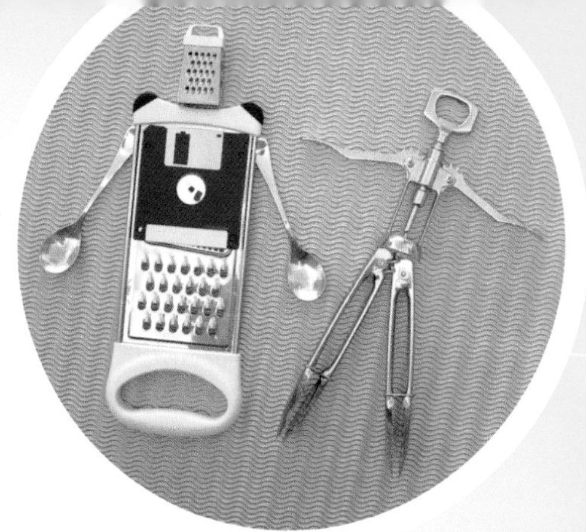

creatures from the cupboard

You can make a sculpture for your yard, balcony, kitchen, or bedroom out of almost anything, and you can probably find all you need in your own home. Look through your kitchen cupboards (check with your grown-ups first) and see if there are any old gadgets that aren't being used anymore. What about old car parts, furniture, or computer stuff? Old saucepan lids in different colors, egg beaters, wooden spoons from the kitchen? Look for pieces of fabric, old clothes, even old shoes. You just need a bit of imagination and some wire or string, and you'll be on your way!

Set up a box to collect bits and pieces that you can turn into art. You'll be reusing, recycling, and creating art all at once!

Photos: Marian Kyte

trash or treasure?

83

Here's another way to reuse paper and recycle it into useful, creative items for your house or for gifts. There's nothing quite like getting your hands into making papier-mâché objects and sculptures. Get creative with old cardboard boxes—make dollhouses, castles, and trains, for a start. Puppets, masks, mobiles, collages, mosaics, hand-made birthday and holiday cards—the list is endless.

Reuse paper products and packaging you find in your house, and make your own gift-wrap and cards for when you give presents. Use papier-mâché to make photo frames, and decorate them with old jewelry, beads, and buttons.

Craft: Marian Kyte, Lachlan and Dixon Chang

84

shake, rattle, and roll

Want a good excuse to get together with your friends and make some noise? (Creative noise, of course.) With a little imagination and things you find hanging around, you can form your very own green band. Think about what kinds of instruments you could make out of old cans, jars, pieces of wood or plastic pipes, and some old nylon fishing line. It's not exactly a new idea—think bluegrass music with its washboards, jugs, and spoons. You can also make traditional instruments such as drums—from a container with fabric or rubber stretched across the opening—and rattles (take-out containers filled with dried beans). What can you do with sticks, reeds, and shells? Use your imagination!

Create your own original musical instrument from existing materials—like a xylophone from empty bottles or a harp from rubber bands and an old can. The possibilities are endless.

Photo: Corbis Australia. Inset: Marian Kyte.

85 color in your garden

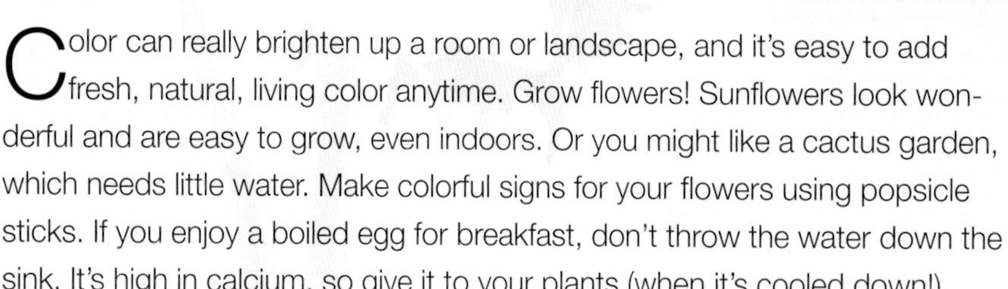

Color can really brighten up a room or landscape, and it's easy to add fresh, natural, living color anytime. Grow flowers! Sunflowers look wonderful and are easy to grow, even indoors. Or you might like a cactus garden, which needs little water. Make colorful signs for your flowers using popsicle sticks. If you enjoy a boiled egg for breakfast, don't throw the water down the sink. It's high in calcium, so give it to your plants (when it's cooled down!).

HERB GARDEN

Decorate your dinner table with fresh flowers instead of plastic ones or other fake materials that may create CO_2 emissions when manufactured. Real flowers look prettier, they smell much nicer, and you can throw them in your compost pile when they wilt!

Photos: Marian Kyte

86

it's only natural

Herbs have been used for centuries in cooking, in cleaning, and to promote good health. You can grow your own herbs, including lavender, peppermint, thyme, and aloe, right at home and use them for many projects, including making teas, soothing lotions, scented potpourri bags, and even bug repellent. You won't be using harmful pesticides and chemicals that might come with store-bought products, and you'll be cutting down on your carbon footprint and creating fun, home-grown products that you can give to family and friends.

Make a fresh herb linen sachet that is also a bug repellent. Go to: http://www.info-galaxy.com/Herbs/Crafts/crafts.html.

Photos: Marian Kyte

87 splashing around

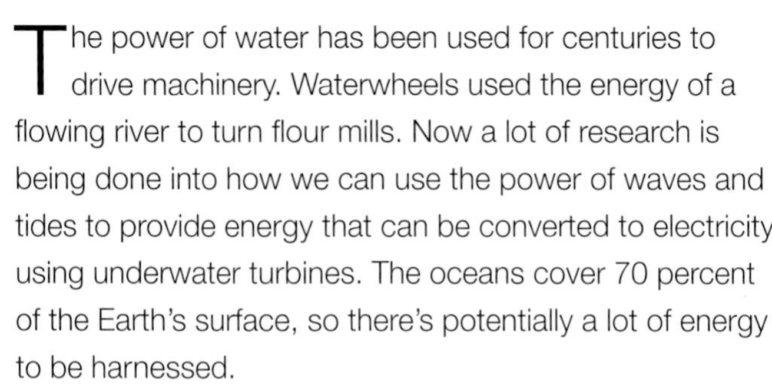

The power of water has been used for centuries to drive machinery. Waterwheels used the energy of a flowing river to turn flour mills. Now a lot of research is being done into how we can use the power of waves and tides to provide energy that can be converted to electricity using underwater turbines. The oceans cover 70 percent of the Earth's surface, so there's potentially a lot of energy to be harnessed.

Learn how we can help keep our planet cleaner by finding new, clean ways to produce energy. Make your own water turbine with an empty milk carton. To learn how, check out www.energyquest.ca.gov/projects/turbine.html.

Photo: Marian Kyte

enjoy the breeze

88

Harnessing the energy of the wind is one way to help reduce greenhouse gases. We've all experienced the power of the wind. It can almost blow you over on a really windy day, but you can have fun with it as well. Flying a kite you've made out of recycled materials is a great way to get a feel for how much energy there is in moving air. It's not surprising that windmills have been used for centuries to drive machinery. If you visit a wind farm and see how large the rotating blades are, it's not hard to imagine how much power there is in the wind and how it can be harnessed to generate clean green electricity.

Fact: Germany produces more electricity from wind power than any other country. Wind power is clean and renewable, unlike coal or oil.

Make a windmill or wind vane for your yard or balcony so you can enjoy the power of the wind. Learn how to do it at http://www.alliantenergykids.com, and go to "wind power toys."

Photo: Corbis Australia

89

the joy of giving

To my best friend

It's always good to give and receive presents. There's something special about gifts that you make yourself—extra special if they're made from recycled materials. You can use old CDs for photo frames, drink coasters, or Christmas tree ornaments; cut up some brightly colored photos from magazines and make mosaic placemats; cook up a storm and make eco-cookies with fresh ingredients from your garden; make gift tags and hand-made wrapping paper from old newspapers, magazines, and junk mail. Then there are houseplants that you can grow from seeds or cuttings … you see, the list really is endless!

Make gift bags out of fabric so they can be used again.

90

what else can I do?

We've given you lots of ideas and information about how to make your world a better place. It's not all gloom and doom. You can have a lot of fun making things better for yourself, your family and friends, and the environment. The future of the world really is in your hands, so why not make a wish list of all the changes you would like to see in the future? Start a journal or diary, and write down your goals. As time goes by, you can compare your wish list with reality. Your journal will be even more special if you use handmade paper—or reuse paper that you already have.

Start your very own eco-blog to let everyone know what you're doing to help save the planet. You can even include pictures of what you've created to inspire others. Send your blog to your local newspaper—they might even make you a regular contributor! Everyone can make a difference—so get started today!

Photo: Marian Kyte and Lachlan Chang

Did you know that U.S. households contribute almost one-fifth of the country's greenhouse gases? So get started now: Take a few simple steps to lower your carbon footprint and make our planet healthier for all living creatures.

true green facts

91 what are greenhouse gases?

The Earth's atmosphere is changing. The build-up of gases released by the burning of fossil fuels, mostly oil and coal, has formed a sort of barrier around the Earth. Water vapor, carbon dioxide, methane, nitrous oxide, and ozone—the greenhouse gases—absorb energy from the sun and stop the heat escaping so that the Earth cannot cool down properly. Carbon dioxide is essential to all forms of life, but too much in the atmosphere is dangerous. It's like sleeping under a heavy blanket in the middle of summer—you overheat. And that's what's happening to the Earth.

Did you know that riding a bike is the most greenhouse-efficient form of transportation? Every gallon of gas your family car does not use saves 1.3 pounds in greenhouse gas pollution.

92

what is carbon dioxide?

Carbon is a chemical that is found in all living things. Coal, graphite, crude oil, and diamonds are almost all carbon. Carbon dioxide, which makes up about 80 percent of greenhouse gases, is a colorless and odorless gas formed from one carbon and two oxygen atoms. Animals breathe CO_2 out, and plants take it in and convert it to oxygen through the process of photosynthesis. When fossil fuels are burned, CO_2 is released into the atmosphere, where it becomes trapped. The delicate balance of the Earth's atmosphere has been upset by human activity. We are cutting down too many trees (deforestation) and releasing too much CO_2 into the atmosphere.

Help check the tire pressure of your family car. Keeping the tires properly inflated can improve your car's gas mileage by more than 3 percent, and for every gallon of gas you save, you keep 20 pounds of CO_2 out of the atmosphere. The tires wear out more slowly, too, if properly inflated.

Photo: Marian Kyte

93

what is global warming?

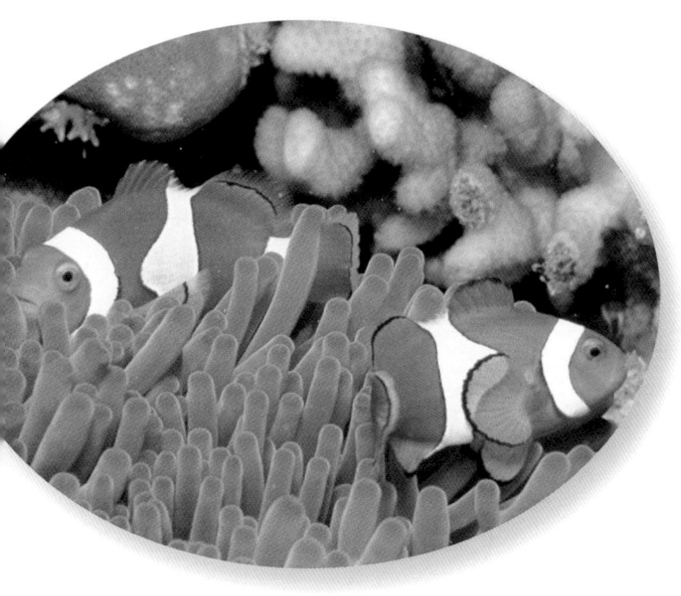

Have you ever been in a greenhouse and noticed how warm and humid it is? The heat gets in through the glass, but it can't escape. That's just what global warming is—the sun's heat is trapped by pollution and greenhouse gases so that the Earth's surface, including the oceans, heats up. As more people on the planet travel, cook, and turn on lights and equipment, more CO_2 is released. It is important that we learn to change our habits. In the United States, most electricity is generated by burning coal, which produces lots of greenhouse gases.

Lower your CO_2 emissions and save electricity—turn off lights you don't need, or wear a sweater instead of turning on the heat—simple ways of doing something about global warming.

Photo: Great Barrier Reef, Tourism Queensland

94

is it too late?

Photo: Daintree, Tourism Queensland

For more than 10,000 years the Earth's temperature has remained at an average of 57°F. But that is changing. The average temperature in the Southern Hemisphere could increase by 2°F by 2010. It doesn't sound like much, but it will have big consequences. The heat is melting the polar ice caps, causing water levels to rise, which will wipe out low-lying islands and coastlines. It is also causing rain levels to drop in some places. If that continues, the Amazon rain forest will lose a lot of the plants that produce oxygen necessary for animals'—and our—survival. But we still have time to save the planet if we act now.

Oceans absorb heat, and the warmer water is endangering marine animals. If you live near water, observe your local shoreline—record the animals you find on the beach or riverbank. Understanding these ecosystems is a step toward understanding the impact of global warming.

high tide

Global warming can cause a rise in sea level in two ways: sea water expanding and polar ice caps melting. It is predicted that global warming will cause significant rises in sea level during this century. Because two-thirds of the world's population live within 50 miles of the coast, this is something to be concerned about. In Bangladesh, for example, a 3-foot rise in sea level would leave more than one-fifth of the country under water, and 10 to 15 million people would lose their homes. Where would they go? Greenland's ice caps are melting faster than scientists predicted, and many species of animal and plant life could soon become extinct. Polar bears need large areas of ice to survive; if the ice caps disappear, so will the polar bears.

Do some research on the Internet or in the library and see how many animals you can find that would be affected by sea level rise and loss of habitat. You might even want to contribute to a not-for-profit group that works to protect animals' habitats.

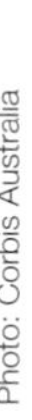

96

extreme weather

In some parts of the world, drought is a terrible problem—for farmers, their livestock, and the economy. With no water to nourish the land, crops can't grow, stock can't survive, food prices increase, and farmers give up. In other parts of the world, ocean storms—hurricanes, typhoons, and cyclones—have grown stronger and more frequent. We don't want more people and cattle in drought-stricken areas to suffer and die. And we don't want extreme weather events such as Hurricane Katrina or raging forest fires to become normal. So we have to stop global warming.

Conduct an experiment that mimics a real-life global warming situation. Half fill a tub or pail with water. Put several large blocks of ice in the tub. Finally, add rocks that are large enough to stick out above the water level. Let the large pieces of ice melt, and see what happens to the water level inside the tub.

Photo: Tourism NSW (photographer unknown)

start right now

97

Photo: Corbis Australia

Act on climate change now. Make it your personal mission to make a difference. Write to your local government officials and tell them why you think creating a sustainable future is important and what you are doing to reduce your carbon footprint at home and at school. It may inspire them. Help reduce the electricity bill at home, and see if your family can change to green power by buying electricity from renewable energy sources. Renewable energy—including solar energy and energy from the wind, waves, and falling water—is increasingly available. It might cost a little more at first, but it will save the planet.

Convince your family to turn down the thermostat just 2 degrees in winter, and turn it up 2 degrees in summer to prevent 2,000 pounds of CO_2 from going into the atmosphere each year—and your family will save nearly $100 on electricity bills!

98

cars of the future

We all now know that SUVs are gas guzzlers! Let's leave them in the rural areas where they may be needed to cross rivers or drive on unpaved roads. They are not really necessary on paved roads. New technology is the future, and hybrid vehicles make good sense. As well as having a gas or diesel engine, these clever cars have a battery and an electric motor to capture and use energy that is normally wasted.

The exhaust that comes from cars is the chief contributor to air pollution in big cities. See if your family can reduce the number of car miles you travel each week by doing these simple things at least one day a week: carpool with neighbors, catch the bus or walk to school, or ride your bike to the local market for that gallon of milk or newspaper.

99

what are governments and businesses doing?

In 1997, most nations of the world signed the Kyoto Protocol—an agreement to work together to reduce carbon emissions. It established target emissions levels for developed countries as well as an emissions trading system, like a carbon stock market, where companies that don't use up their "pollution allowance" can sell some of it to companies that pollute more.

Set up a carbon trading card system. Make a card for every energy-saving activity, and give it a point score. Turning off a light might earn 1 point, walking or biking instead of being driven might earn 5 points, and eating local or organic food might earn 3 points. Eating processed food or buying a toy with lots of packaging might cost you points. Trade cards with your friends so that you can help each other go green and have fun, too.

Photo: Corbis Australia

100

and the answer is?

We need to find ways to reduce our reliance on fossil fuels for our energy needs. The four Rs are part of the solution, but the other part is new technology. Individuals and companies all over the world are working on ways to produce green energy and products that are easy on the environment. Who knows, you might be the one who comes up with the next great invention for a sustainable energy source that doesn't produce carbon emissions.

Why not think about devoting your future to the environment? There are many industries, and more emerging all the time, that offer jobs where you can make a real and lasting positive impact on the environment. Learn about these jobs by talking to the grown-ups in your life or going on the Internet or to your library. The future is in your hands—use your imagination.

Photo: Corbis Australia

Photo top left: Marian Kyte
All other photos: Chris Bennett

cool resources >

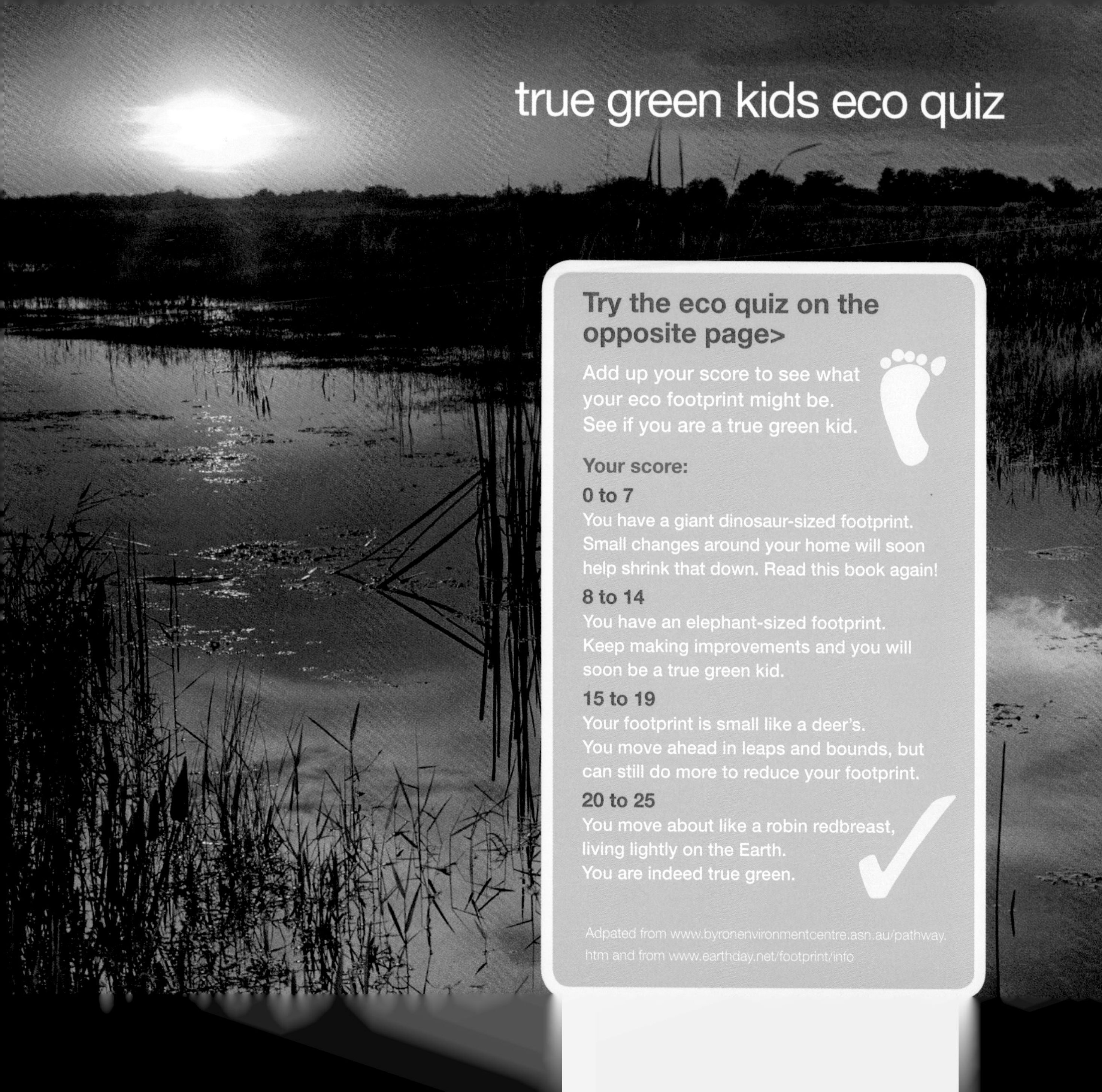

Try the eco quiz on the opposite page>

Add up your score to see what your eco footprint might be. See if you are a true green kid.

Your score:

0 to 7
You have a giant dinosaur-sized footprint. Small changes around your home will soon help shrink that down. Read this book again!

8 to 14
You have an elephant-sized footprint. Keep making improvements and you will soon be a true green kid.

15 to 19
Your footprint is small like a deer's. You move ahead in leaps and bounds, but can still do more to reduce your footprint.

20 to 25
You move about like a robin redbreast, living lightly on the Earth. You are indeed true green.

Adpated from www.byronenvironmentcentre.asn.au/pathway.htm and from www.earthday.net/footprint/info

For each environmental topic, choose one statement that best describes you.
Write down your ratings in the subtotal boxes and add up your score!

your rating	be a true green kid	waste	energy	water	biodiversity
5>	I really enjoy the taste of fresh organic food. I feel healthy when I eat it.	We have a compost bin at home and school and we help our neighbors with their food scraps, too.	I catch public transportation to school, walk, or car pool with other families.	We have a rainwater tank and use recycled water on the yard or on our potted plants at home. We have a water-efficient shower head.	Our street/my school is planting a community garden/ vegetable patch.
4>	At home we try to use chemical-free detergent, cleaning products, and shampoo.	I look after the worm farm and feed the worms food scraps.	At home we have a solar hot water heater.	We wash the family car with recycled water or water from the rainwater tank.	My family has planted native plants in the yard.
3>	I help my family in the yard or with our potted plants. Gardening can be fun.	When we go shopping I remind everyone to take the reusable bags.	I turn the computer or TV off when I've finished using them. We have swapped the light bulbs for new fluorescent lights at home.	I take 4-minute showers. We have a timer on the shower wall.	I want to build a bird house so that local birds will come to visit.
2>	We wash the car on the grass so we don't pollute the storm water, or we go to the car wash.	We make sure that we use the correct colored recycling bins.	I turn the lights off when I leave the room.	We follow our town's water restrictions.	We might plant more native shrubs and trees in the yard.
1>	I want to live a more eco-friendly life, but I haven't started yet.	We fill up our garbage can with garbage bags every week and sometimes forget to recycle.	I know that global warming is real, and we need to reduce our electricity use, but we haven't started yet.	I realize that using excess water is wasteful, but I often forget.	We just have a lawn or patio. I'm too busy for plants.
0>	We haven't thought much about the environment at home.	We don't recycle.	We have lots of big appliances, which is fine with us.	Water doesn't cost much, so we leave the tap running when that's the easiest thing to do.	We let our pets roam the streets and yard at night.
subtotal >					

websites

water

Drink tap	http://www.drinktap.org/kidsdnn	water use statistics, fun quizzes
Water calculator	ans.engr.wisc.edu/eic/waterform.html	personal water impact calculator
Water facts	http://www.epa.gov/safewater/kids/waterfactsoflife.html	games and activities
Interactive water house tour	www.getwise.org	send a free "Get Wise" e-card to friends
Be waterwise	www.bewaterwise.com	tips for getting serious about saving water

recycling

Freecycle	www.freecycle.org	online free swap site
Recycling revolution	www.recycling-revolution.com	everything you want to know about recycling
All about recycling	www.earth911.org/recycling/	a to z about recycling
Cell phone recycling	www.wirelessrecycling.com	everything you need to know about recycling your mobile phone
	www.eco-cell.org	recycle your mobile phone and help others at the same time; e-waste recycling listing
Ink jet printer cartridges	www.enviro-smart.com	recycle used ink jet printer cartridges
Computer disks	www.greendisk.com	recycling computer disks and computer-related waste
Battery recycling	www.ehso.com/ehshome/batteries.php	household battery site

energy

Kids saving energy	www.eere.energy.gov/kids/	games, tips, facts, and quizzes
Be an energy star!	www.energystar.gov/index.cfm?c=kids.kids_index	great interactive kids' site
Become an "energy hog buster"	http://www.energyhog.org/childrens.htm	"hog and seek" game, scavenger hunt, and more

food

Organic farming	www.localharvest.org	all about local, organic foods
Sustainable table	www.sustainabletable.org	lots of information about sustainable food
Organic foods explanation	http://www.mayoclinic.com/health/organic-food/NU00255	organic foods and your health
Organic foods and kids	http://www.thedietchannel.com/organic-food-and-kids	information about ingredients

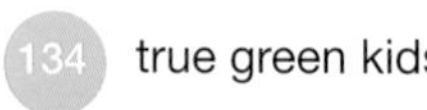

Consumer reports buying organic	http://www.consumerreports.org/cro/food/diet-nutrition/organic-products/organic-products-206/overview/	good tips for buying quality organic foods
Sustainable seafood guide	www.endangeredfishalliance.org	how you can help our oceans in crisis and order a sustainable seafood guide

schools

Alliance to save energy	www.ase.org	save energy at school
EPA schools site	www.epa.gov/climatechange/wycd/school.html	how your school can make a difference
Walk-to-school program	www.walktoschool.org	make this happen at your school
Edible schoolyard	www.esynola.org	inspiration for a school-based gardening program
School compost or worm farm	www.pbskids.org/dragonflytv/show/wormfarm.html	how to get started
The green squad	www.nrdc.org/greensquad/	a how-to guide for students to help green their schools
Earth matters 4 kids	www.Earthmatters4kids.org/	bring a virtual natural world into the classroom
Clean up activities	http://www.cleanup.org.au/au/Kids/	activities from recycling to cleaning up

garden

Eco backyards	www.ecobackyard.com	ideas, tips, and information for urban and backyard gardening
Sustainable gardening	www.sustainable-gardening.com	everything from garden predators to sustainable garden centers
Energy-efficient landscaping	http://www.eere.energy.gov/consumer/your_home/landscaping/	how to save energy with smart landscaping
Urban gardening	http://www.urbangardeninghelp.com/	the joys of gardening in an urban landscape

pets

Taking care of pets	http://pbskids.org/itsmylife/family/pets/article7.html	all about having healthy pets
Caring for animals	http://www.aspca.org/site/PageServer?pagename=kids_home	how to choose and care for a pet

gifts/shopping

Books	http://www.theweathermakers.org/	news, tips, information, cartoons, and more
More books	www.childsake.com	young adult version, teaching resources

websites

Planet-friendly products	www.planetfriendly.com	order bulk copies for your school
Eco-conscious shopping	www.taraluna.com/	products and news
Shop with companies that care	www.climatecounts.org	list of environmentally responsible companies

vacation/travel

Check out our national parks	http://www.nps.gov	national park service site
Travel smart	http://www.terrapass.com/	reduce and balance your impact; travel calculators, carbon offsets
Special places	whc.unesco.org	world heritage sites
The nature conservancy	www.nature.org/aboutus/travel/ecotourism/	eco-tourism info
Dolphin research	www.dolphins.org	find out all about dolphins and other marine mammals

green groups

Clean up the world	http://www.cleanuptheworld.org	find out how an Australian idea is helping other countries
Earth911	www.earth911.org/for-students	facts, information, tips, and activities for students and teachers on saving the Earth
Save our rainforests	www.rainforest-alliance.org/	great ideas for global conservation
Environmental defense fund	http://www.edf.org	all kinds of tips and information for living green
Earth day	www.2earthday.net	how people come together to make positive change
Charities	www.eco-usa.net/orgs/index.shtml	listing of all U.S. environmental groups by state
Greenpeace	http://www.greenpeace.org	a voice for this fragile Earth and the creatures who inhabit it
Audubon society	www.audubonintl.org	ways to protect and sustain our natural resources
Abundant forests alliance	www.plantitforward.com	all about certified sustainable forests and products
Natural resources defense council	www.nrdc.org/makewaves/	complete kids site on helping the planet
Planet ark	http://www.planetark.org	reduce your impact on the planet—news, pictures, campaigns
Nature conservancy	www.nature.org	lots of good information about preserving the Earth's biodiversity
World wildlife fund	www.wwf.org	adopt an animal or volunteer for a local project
Governmental resources	www.ehso.com/govtenvirsites.php	comprehensive list of all U.S. government environmental websites
Energy star	http://www.energystar.gov	find out more about standby power

Consumer's guide to energy efficiency	www.eere.energy.gov/consumer/	all about saving energy and using renewable energy
U.S. environmental protection agency	http://www.epa.gov	a to z on the environment—information, news, regulations, and more

science

Ecological footprint	http://www.ecofoot.org	choose your country and language for the quiz
Safe climate calculator	http://www.safeclimate.net/calculator	check the size of your household's carbon footprint
Carbon offsets, green power	http://www.carbonfund.org	all about carbon offsets
Carbon footprint calculator	http://www.myfootprint.org	quiz to calculate your carbon footprint
Footprint calculator	http://www.zerofootprintkids.com	designed for kids and includes food, water, and trash information

fun & learning

Living green	www.thegreenguide.com	weekly pointers about how to be green
National parks junior ranger program	www.nps.gov/learn/juniorranger.htm	become a junior park ranger
Environmental kids' club	www.epa.gov/kids/	a fun environmental "A-to-Z" site for kids and teachers
Sustainable living	www.eartheasy.com/article_enviro_sites_kids.htm	all about sustainable living
Kids go wild	www.kidsgowild.com	learn about wild animals and how to protect them
Kids planet	www.kidsplanet.org	complete listing with information on endangered species; adopt-an-animal; teachers' guides
National geographic	http://www.kids.nationalgeographic.com/	lots of activities for kids
Planet slayer	www.abc.net.au/science/planetslayer/	fun cartoons, a "save the earth" adventure game
Say no to plastic bags	http://www.droptheplasticbag.org	facts about plastic bags and how to get rid of them
All-kids global warming aite	http://www.planetpatrol.info	an eco-website made by kids, for kids
Stop global warming	www.stopglobalwarming.msn.org	global warming news; see athletes and celebrities talk about global warming
Be a global warming investigator	http://www.adventureecology.com	eco-adventure game of global warming spots
Campaign earth	http://www.campaignearth.org	tips for living a greener lifestyle
Earth day activities	http://greenliving.lovetoknow.com	Earth Day activities for kids
No impact man	http://www.noimpactman.com	a man and his family trying to make no impact on the environment. Can he do it?
Nature challenge for kids	www.davidsuzuki.org/kids/	simple and fun things to do to protect nature

glossary

biodegradable> describes something that can decay and be broken down by living organisms, such as bacteria, or by sunlight. For example, food scraps can be broken down and turned into compost and used as a fertilizer.

biodiversity> "bio" means "life," so "biodiversity" means the great variety of living things that exist on the planet. All life is interconnected, so we must do all we can to maintain as many species as possible.

carbon dioxide (CO_2)> a colorless gas that has no smell and is made up of one atom of carbon and two atoms of oxygen. All animals, including humans, breathe out CO_2, and plants breathe it in to produce oxygen. It is also produced when fossil fuels are burnt to create energy. When too much CO_2 gets trapped in the Earth's atmosphere, it causes the Earth to heat up.

carbon footprint> how we measure the amount of greenhouse gas produced by the things we do. It is usually measured in tons of carbon dioxide emitted into the atmosphere every year.

carbon neutral> doing things that reduce and offset the amount of greenhouse gas we produce. For example, switching to green power, recycling, walking to school instead of driving, and planting trees.

carbon offset> it is possible to make up for some emissions from cars and planes by supporting renewable energy activities, such as programs that invest in solar or wind power, or programs that plant large numbers of trees that absorb gases like CO_2 and breathe out oxygen.

carbon sequestration> a process that reduces CO_2 in the atmosphere by collecting CO_2 and storing it underground so it is not released into the atmosphere; it also occurs naturally through plant photosynthesis. This is why keeping as many forests alive and planting more trees is good for the planet.

carbon sink> trees, the oceans, and soil can all absorb CO_2 and stop it from being released back into the atmosphere.

carbon trading> companies that release CO_2 into the atmosphere can buy "carbon credits" from others that don't, such as tree-planting programs. The aim is to balance the amount of harmful gases being released. It costs more for those who release CO_2, while the seller makes money from the deal so they can expand their activities and further help the environment. These markets operate like a stock market and are well-established in Europe and the United States.

climate change> changes to the climate of the Earth caused by global warming. This happens when too much CO_2 and other greenhouse gases get into the atmosphere and trap the heat from the sun, which would normally be able to escape. It is now widely accepted that this has been caused by human activity.

compact fluorescent lights (CFLs)> a new kind of light bulb that helps to reduce energy use. CFLs are the same as the well-known fluorescent tubes, but smaller and a different shape. They use less energy and don't produce as much heat as the standard incandescent bulbs and last up to ten times as long.

dioxin> the popular name for a group of extremely dangerous organic compounds that can accumulate in the body tissue of humans and animals.

eco-friendly> "eco" means "ecology" —the study of living things and how they interact—so "eco-friendly" means something that does no harm to life or to the environment.

ecological footprint> a measure of how much land is needed to provide everything a person, group, city, or country uses. This amount of land also needs to absorb the waste that is created. People living in wealthy societies use more and create more waste than those living in poorer countries, so they have a larger ecological footprint.

ecotourism> a form of tourism that makes sure the environment is not harmed in any way by tourists. It focuses on natural places and aims to provide ways tourists can enjoy the environment and learn how to look after it.

environmental audit> an assessment of the environmental impact that a person or organization has on the environment.

e-waste> all those old bits of electrical equipment such as mobile phones, computers, DVD players, and cables that people throw away.

fossil fuels> carbon deposits in the Earth that were made by billions of animals and plants that lived many thousands of years ago. Over time they are converted into coal, gas and oil. Once we have used them all up, there will be no more fossil fuels for millions of years.

global warming> When there is too much CO_2 and other greenhouse gases in the Earth's atmosphere, the heat from the sun cannot escape, so the atmosphere gets hotter—just like a greenhouse that is used for growing plants that need warmth and humidity.

greenhouse gas> any atmospheric gas that contributes to the greenhouse effect by absorbing energy from the sun. Naturally occurring gases include water vapor, carbon dioxide, methane, nitrous oxide, and ozone. Human activities, like generating electricity in coal-fired power stations, add to these gases.

green power> electricity generated from renewable sources such as water, wind, and solar power that do not emit greenhouse gases.

hybrid engine> an engine that has more than one source of power; usually a gasoline engine and an electric motor that work together more efficiently. It can get up to 60 miles per hour.

Kyoto Protocol> an international agreement on global warming and emissions targets set at the United Nations Conference on Climate Change in Kyoto, Japan, in 1997. The United States is the only industrialized nation who has not signed it.

landfill> garbage that is buried in the ground between layers of dirt. It can take many years to break down, and the process produces methane. It sometimes gives off dangerous chemicals that can cause pollution, especially if they get into water sources.

methane> a gas with a greenhouse effect 23 times greater than carbon dioxide. Methane is produced naturally from things like volcanoes, wetlands, termites, and the ocean. A lot also comes from human activity, such as the decomposition of organic garbage buried in landfills and from cattle and sheep passing gas.

organic> refers to something that is produced naturally, without fertilizers made from fossil fuels, artificial pesticides, or genetically modified crop varieties.

oxygen> makes up one-fifth of the air we breathe. It is a colorless, tasteless gas with no smell. All living things need it to live. The oxygen we breathe today was first formed millions of years ago by the earliest species of plant life in the oceans.

photosynthesis> the process plants use to live; sunlight converts water and CO_2 into food for the plant; oxygen is released as a waste product.

plastic code> a number identifying the plastic type in a product or packaging. All plastics marked 1 to 7 are recyclable, though in practice many are not: 1 > polyethylene terephthalate (PET); 2> high density polyethylene (HDPE); 3> unplasticized polyvinyl chloride (UPVC) or plasticized polyvinyl chloride (PPVC); 4> low density polyethylene (LDPE): 5> polypropylene (PP); 6> polystyrene (PS) or expandable polystyrene (EPS); 7> other, including nylon and acrylic.

renewable energy> energy that is produced from natural sources like the wind, the sun, or water and not fossil fuels.

solar-powered> a method of making power by turning sunlight into electricity.

sustainability> the ability to provide what is needed now without using up resources that can't be replaced.

waste management> reducing the amount of garbage going into landfills, through efficient use of materials, reducing waste, and recycling or reusing discarded materials.

Clean Up the World

Clean Up the World, the international outreach campaign of Clean Up Australia, was co-founded by True Green creator, Kim McKay, and Ian Kiernan, AO—legendary solo yachtsman and 1994 Australian of the Year.

In partnership with the United Nations Environment Programme (UNEP), Clean Up the World annually attracts more than 35 million volunteers who join community-led initiatives to clean up, fix up, and conserve their local environment.

Sixteen years after its launch, the campaign has become a successful action program that spans some 120 countries, encouraging communities to take control of their own destiny by improving the health of their community and environment.

Global activities include waste collection, education campaigns, environmental concerts, creative competitions and exhibitions on improving water quality, planting trees, minimizing waste, reducing greenhouse gas emissions, and establishing recycling centers.

Look for how you can plot your Clean Up the World activity on Google Maps, or visit the Clean Up the World website to find out how your school, community, company, or organization can become involved:
www.cleanuptheworld.org

"We can all make a difference and joining in Clean Up the World is a simple and practical way to do something about global warming and climate change. Be part of it and help Clean Up Our Climate!"

Ian Kiernan, AO, Founder and Chairman, Clean Up the World

About Adventure Ecology

What we do is fueled by what we feel most strongly about: adventure and ecology.

We read the headlines, saw TV reports, and listened to scientists talk about our Earth's health crisis. So rather than bury our heads in the sand, we decided to tackle the situation head-on and hands-on.

Adventure Ecology inspires a planet-friendly attitude. There's no need to unpack that green superhero cape, stop wearing deodorant, or chain yourself to a tree! It's about being in tune with our planet through our everyday activities and feeling empowered to make a difference.

Our planet isn't getting any younger or healthier. Like your favorite t-shirt or goldfish, all things that age require care, respect, and protection.

And when you're doing it alongside millions of others worldwide, you can't help but feel inspired.

At Adventure Ecology, passion and adventure are in our blood. Are you ready to jump in and achieve your own mission possible for our planet?

Join Adventure Ecology:
www.adventureecology.com

David de Rothschild
Founder, Adventure Ecology;
National Geographic Emerging Explorer;
and Clean Up the World Ambassador

Photo: Marc Stanley, titomedia

Kim McKay (right) is the co-founder and deputy chairwoman of Clean Up Australia and Clean Up the World. She is an international social and sustainability marketing consultant who counts National Geographic among her clients.

Jenny Bonnin (left) is a director of Clean Up Australia and Clean Up the World. She and Kim are partners in the social and sustainability marketing firm, Momentum2. Together, they created the True Green brand. Jenny has two children and two step-children.

Previous books in the True Green series: *True Green: 100 Everyday Ways You Can Contribute to a Healthier Planet* (NG Books, April 2007) and *True Green @ Work: 100 Ways You Can Make the Environment Your Business,* with business writer Tim Wallace (NG Books, February 2008). Look for *True Green Home* in 2009.

Russell Thomson worked for many years as a performer, producer, and manager in theater for young people, before evolving into a writer, editor, and proofreader. After several years working for a major children's publisher, he now freelances through his company, Clear Communications.

Marian Kyte is a freelance designer with a passion for incorporating sustainability principles into her work. Her clients have included Qantas, Craftsman House Books, Power Publications, Sherman Galleries, Art & Australia, Limelight magazine, and True Green. Her son Locky is her inspiration.

acknowledgments

True Green Kids is a true team effort, and we certainly had a lot of fun brainstorming and working together to produce this happy book. Working with Marian Kyte again is a joy. Her eye for detail and ability to communicate with images and color is a real gift. Where would we be without her to make our ideas come alive? We thank Russell Thomson, the wordsmith who cut pages into paragraphs, managing to say the same thing but in the right language, and to photographers Kathryn Whitney Lucey and Chris Bennett, who captured the kids so delightfully. Special thanks to our very special friend and colleague, Kathy Stark, who reversioned the text for the U.S. market and who continues to work hard every day for the benefit of our community and our planet. Thanks also to Nancy Feresten of National Geographic Children's Books for her excellent editing and suggestions, and the whole team at National Geographic Books.

We salute Ian Kiernan, who is our inspiration at Clean Up, and who works every minute of every day to help us all understand that we need to change the way we live in order to leave the planet in a healthy state for our children and grandchildren. Thanks, too, to the dedicated team at Clean Up the World for their incredible efforts.

We dedicate this book to the children in our extended families: Kim's niece, Bec, and nephews Matt and David; Jenny's children Mark, Jane, Shaun, and Eliot; and Ian's beautiful grandchildren, Saskia, Madelaine, Amelia, Louis, and Tom, as well as Kathy's fantastic kids Michael and Maggie.

And a special mention for Lachlan Chang and his friends, who were central to this project.

Now it's up to you—the True Green Kids of the USA!

*"If you want to go fast, go alone;
if you want to go far, go together."*

African proverb quoted by Al Gore
when he accepted the 2007 Nobel Peace Prize

Photo: Chris Bennett